SAP® APO® System Administration

 **PRESS**

SAP PRESS and SAP Technical Support Guides are issued by
Bernhard Hochlehnert, SAP AG

SAP PRESS is a joint initiative of SAP and Galileo Press. The know-how offered by SAP specialists combined with the expertise of the publishing house
Galileo Press offers the reader expert books in the field. SAP PRESS features
first-hand information and expert advice, and provides useful skills for pro-
fessional decision-making.

SAP PRESS offers a variety of books on technical and business related topics
for the SAP user. For further information, please visit our website:
www.sap-press.com.

Sigrid Hagemann, Liane Will
SAP R/3 System Administration
2003, approx. 450 pp., ISBN 1-59229-014-4

Horst Keller, Joachim Jacobitz
ABAP Objects - The Official Reference
2 volumes and CD set
2003, 1056 pp., ISBN 1-59229-011-6

Paul Read
SAP Database Administration
with Microsoft SQL Server 2000
2002, 384 pp., ISBN 1-59229-005-1

Helmut Stefani
Archiving Your SAP Data
A comprehensive guide to plan and execute archiving projects
2003, 334 pp., ISBN 1-59229-008-6

Werner Hertleif, Christoph Wachter
SAP Smart Forms
Creating forms quickly and easily - no programming required!
2003, approx. 450 pp., ISBN 1-59229-010-8

Liane Will

SAP® APO® System Administration

Principles for effective APO System Management

Translation: Lemoine International, Inc.,
Salt Lake City, UT
Proofreading: J.J. Andrews
Cover Design: department, Cologne, Ger-
many
Printed in Germany

ISBN 1-59229-012-4

Contents

Foreword to the series of books

At SAP AG, our first priority is to ensure that the SAP software solutions in your enterprise run successfully and at a minimal cost. This "Lowest Cost of Ownership" is achieved with fast and efficient implementation, together with optimal and dependable operation. SAP Active Global Support is actively and consistently there to help you, with the new SAP Solution Management strategy. Throughout the entire lifecycle of a solution, SAP offers customers all necessary services, first-class support, a suitable infrastructure, and the relevant know-how. The new strategy is backed up by three powerful support programs: *Safeguarding*, or, in other words, risk management; *Solution Management Optimization*, which aims to optimize the customer's IT solution; and *Empowering*, which ensures a targeted, effective transfer of knowledge from SAP to the customer.

The imparting of knowledge is also one of the key aims of this book—part of the line of *SAP Technical Support Guides*. This series gives you a detailed overview of technical aspects and concepts for managing SAP software solutions. The topics dealt with in these books range from a technical implementation project to running a software system and the relevant database system.

Whether you are new to SAP system management or wish to gain further qualifications, you will benefit from the wealth of practical experience and first-hand information contained in these books. With this line of books, SAP also endeavors to help prepare you for qualification as a "Certified Technical Consultant". Please note, however: These books cannot replace, nor do they attempt to replace, personal experience gained from working with the various SAP solutions! Rather, the authors offer suggestions to help in your day-to-day work with the software. Innovation in SAP solutions always brings with it new challenges and solutions for system management. The demands made on the customer's own or external support organizations also increase. The expertise and knowledge of these organizations can be a great help in avoiding problems when using the software. Therefore, one of the core tasks of this series of books is to teach problem-solving skills.

Even in this Internet age, books prove to be an ideal medium for imparting knowledge in a compact form. Furthermore, their content complements the new service and support platform, the SAP Solution Manager, and other new services offered by SAP. The series provides background knowledge on the operation and functioning of new SAP solutions and contributes to customer satisfaction.

Gerhard Oswald
Member of the executive board of SAP AG

Dr. Uwe Hommel
Senior Vice President at SAP AG
SAP Active Global Support

Rot, March 2003

Preface

With the growth in the range of software offered by SAP, the tasks in system administration have also been extended and changed. It is no longer a question of managing individual R/3 systems; instead, you now have to work with entire system landscapes, in which the systems exchange data from one system to the other. One of the new software solutions from SAP AG is the *Advanced Planner and Optimizer* (APO) for Supply Chain Management. APO software uses the same basis as R/3 software, but includes new components. Most system administration tools can be used in the APO system in the same way as they are used in R/3. There are also tasks specific to APO systems, given its particular architecture and application.

When I was taking my first steps to integrate an APO system into a system landscape, Philip Klingenburg, who unfortunately is not around to see this book, was there to help me. I came to the conclusion that a book on APO system administration would be very useful for the operator. I therefore set myself the challenge of producing a book on APO system administration, comparable to what was available for R/3 system administration. This book contains a mass of know-how and a wealth of experience for operating APO 3.1 with liveCache 7.4. It also makes reference to APO 3.0 and liveCache 7.2.

I would like to thank my colleagues who have helped me in many respects, not merely in writing this book. In particular, I would like to thank Jochen Bergmann, Jochen Hartmann, Steffen Hoffmann, Georg Klinger, Dr. Lars Mihan, Helga Neumann, Günther Pecht-Seibert, Jürgen Primsch, Wiegand Schulz, Dimitri Smolkin, Ralf Sosnitzka, Werner Thesing, and Dr. Martin Voss for their contributions to this book. Thanks are also due to my former colleague Augustinus Wohlfart, who unfortunately passed away recently. He was a key figure in the conception and development of this series of books. I would also like to mention Dr. Gerhard Paulin and Manfred Hagen, without whose help I may never have written books at all.

And last but by no means least, I would like to thank my family for their encouragement and for giving me the space I needed when putting this book together.

Liane Will
SAP Active Global Support

Berlin, March 2003

Introduction

APO software is the Supply Chain Management solution developed by SAP AG. Supply Chain Management represents the integration and optimization of logistics processes that go beyond enterprise boundaries, and, therefore, the need to provide and process complex and diverse data. Due to the complexity of managing supply chains, the architecture of the APO system differs significantly from the technology you will know from R/3 systems. R/3 software is based on client/server architecture, which is made up of a database, instances, and front-end software. APO software is also based on client/server architecture. In contrast to the SAP R/3 system, however, not only is data stored in relational structures in the relational database management system (RDBMS), but the data that is relevant to planning is managed in the liveCache in an object-oriented way. The liveCache is a completely new component in software systems, the like of which has not been seen on the market before now.

Last but not least, this innovative new architectural element means that an APO system operates differently from an R/3 system. However, much of what you know about R/3 can also be transferred to an APO system. In order to understand this book on APO system administration, the reader should be familiar with the following topics:

▶ Client-server architecture and configuration
▶ Change and transport management
▶ Users and authorizations
▶ Background processing
▶ Updates
▶ Output configuration and management
▶ Data distribution and data transfer
▶ System monitoring
▶ Database administration

Based on this background knowledge, *SAP APO System Administration* sets out to describe the details of operating an APO system and integrating it into the existing system landscape. More than just the different architecture and new software components need to be taken into account in the administration of an APO system. When you implement an APO system, an intensive exchange of data is also initiated between the linked systems.

As a result, it is no longer sufficient to merely consider the operation of one individual system; you need to keep an eye on the overall operation of all systems involved.

When you implement an APO system, the operation of existing R/3 systems is also affected. Monitoring the interface between the APO and R/3 systems is particularly critical to the operation of the system landscape. This book describes the new or amended tasks involved in administering a system landscape with the SAP R/3 and APO systems.

Chapter 1, "Application Overview", gives an introduction to the application solutions that are possible with APO software. Unlike R/3 solutions, with APO, the application solution implemented has an effect on administrative operation.

Chapter 2, "APO Software", provides an introduction to the components of APO and how they should be maintained. You will also learn about scalability in an APO system.

The integration of an APO system into the system landscape is presented in **Chapter 3**, "The APO System in the System Landscape". An important task of system administration is monitoring the exchange of data between the APO system and assigned systems. This chapter also describes the tools available for problem solving, and how to use them.

The liveCache, a new component of APO software, is the main focus of **Chapter 4**, "liveCache Architecture". It presents the essential features, concepts, and processes of the architecture.

The tools and administration tasks that are used in conjunction with the liveCache are presented in **Chapter 5**, "liveCache Administration Tools". The use of these tools is demonstrated with the help of some typical problem cases.

Chapter 6, "LCApps (COM Routines)", deals with the technology of COM routines—or LCApps, as they are now called. In APO systems, application logic transferred is not only by ABAP programs, but also by COM routines. This should be taken into account when analyzing the operation of APO systems.

For an APO system, backup and recovery is more complex than for an R/3 system. The liveCache requires a backup concept of its own. **Chapter 7**, "Backup and Recovery", deals with this subject.

When data is transferred between components and systems, the question of consistency between them arises. In **Chapter 8**, "Consistency Checks", the tools available for checking and restoring consistency are described.

Optimizers can be used for specific planning steps in the management of the logistics chain. They are also a new component that is not used in R/3 systems. **Chapter 9**, "Optimizers", shows which tools are used to operate optimizers.

Chapter 10, "Authorizations", gives a brief introduction to the area of authorizations in APO systems. The main focus is on the authorizations used for system administration.

Chapter 11, "Performance Monitoring and Tuning", covers the important aspects of performance and tools for performance optimization.

1 Application Overview

This chapter gives an overview of the most important application modules of APO and how they are used. It presents the technical challenges and requirements that arise for the system administrator as a result of using these modules.

1.1 Business Content

The abbreviation APO stands for *Advanced Planner and Optimizer*. APO is the SAP software for *Supply Chain Management* (SCM). With SCM, unlike the SAP R/3 system, it is important that the system administrator understands the concepts and purpose of the application and the essential features of the application flow. Before going into the technical aspects of implementing SCM with APO, we would first like to introduce you to the basic concepts of SCM.

SCM is designed to integrate and optimize cross-enterprise logistics processes. These processes includes areas such as production and transport planning, as well as material requirements and distribution planning. The capacities and time limits of the parties involved in the logistics chain are taken into account (see Figure 1.1).

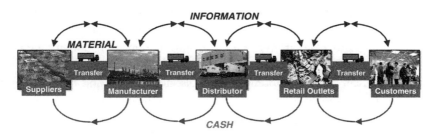

Figure 1.1 Logistics chain

All necessary planning data is processed in real time. The aim of SCM is to achieve the best customer orientation for the lowest cost. The technical execution and establishment of SCM in an enterprise opens brand-new possibilities in logistics. To clearly understand these new possibilities, let us first take a look back over the development of planning technology in software.

Some of the first planning-related technology was material requirements planning, based on bills of materials. The bills of materials were broken

MRP

down into their constituent parts and orders were generated from this. Deadline requirements and limits on capacity were not taken into account. This procedure was known as *Material Resource Planning* (MRP). This relatively simple procedure was later extended and became MRP II, in which production resources were also taken into account. Further planning runs could be linked sequentially with limits on capacity and deadlines. However, other planning systems had to be consulted for planning beyond the boundaries of a particular plant or beyond the boundaries of an enterprise. Another disadvantage of MRP II was that planning periods were relatively long. The sequential processing of the individual steps also resulted in longer lead times before conclusive MRP II results were available. The results were obsolete before they arrived. MRP II could not fully represent the dynamic of a logistics chain because the different components and resources were constantly flowing in.

ERP *Enterprise Resource Planning* (ERP) marked a significant improvement, and it could also be used in the SAP R/3 system. The decisive advantage of ERP systems is the integration of all significant areas of business, such as accounting, HR, and controlling. The boundaries between the individual modules are flexible and allow for active data exchange. This strength is central to the success of the SAP R/3 system.

The increasing interconnection between individual enterprises not only calls for the integration of all the data of an enterprise, but also results in cross-enterprise planning tasks. SCM was the first to be able to deal with these complex logistics chains. It can be used to handle internal and external logistics processes from the areas of production, transport, requirements, and distribution planning, from the supplier right through to the end user. SCM also has optimization tools, aggregation and monitoring functions, and the flexibility necessary to deal with changes in the logistics chain. The exchange of data between these components is active and goes in both directions—that is to say, information is brought together in SCM and the results are sent back to the source systems. SCM is the coordinating intersection in a logistics chain.

From a technical point of view, SCM software is superior to the ERP systems used. Maintenance of master data is carried out as before in the ERP systems. Information on availability, lead time, or requirements is passed on to the SCM system through the APO software. Currently, software solutions are required for help with planning for more than just a company and its components; the trend is to include business partners in the planning process. The obvious step is to develop from previously local SCM to cross-enterprise planning of the logistics chain, with the help of the Internet. The aim is to synchronize an entire network. This is referred to as *Supply Chain Collaboration* or *Collaborative Planning* (CLP). APO software from SAP offers an Internet connection for CLP, as well as the corresponding functions.

1.2 Application Module

APO is made up of the following application areas:

1.2.1 Demand Planning (DP)

Demand Planning allows you to forecast customer demand on the basis of different historical and statistical forecasting methods. The actual forecasting methods can in turn be developed with the help of APO and other software.

At first, DP uses primarily the mathematical-statistical forecasting methods provided in APO software. Experience and historical data, such as data already available in the R/3 or BW systems (*Business Information Warehouse*), make it possible to fine-tune the forecasting methods, and to adapt them to suit particular products or particular customers. DP is based on a planning horizon of 6 to 24 months. The process of calculating demand is called a *planning run*, and in the case of DP, it is also referred to as the *forecast run*. The results of a planning run can be revised manually; for example, promotion campaigns which increase demand may be planned. Once the forecast is complete, the data is passed on to *Supply Network Planning* (SNP). DP can even be used to make broad estimates of demand for a product in the future. These demands are not based on any concrete customer demand; therefore, they are referred to as *anonymous demands*.

1.2.2 Supply Network Planning (SNP)

SNP is based on a planning horizon of 4 to 8 weeks. Demand planned in DP is set against the capacities of individual factories. Can the plan created in DP be realized with the resources available (materials, machines, manpower, and so on)? Existing customer orders are also taken into account, and we can therefore speak of concrete demands. In contrast to anonymous demands, concrete demands can be linked to a customer order. In most cases, however, it is not enough to merely check that the Demand Planning done in DP can be covered by production. The objective is to optimally distribute the production necessary to fulfill the plan over different plants (*locations*). The planning run used to determine how this production work should be distributed is known as the *SNP run*. APO 3.0 supports three basic methods of the SNP run.

SNP Heuristics

SNP heuristics is an infinite planning method, which means that only the basic capacity of resources is taken into account: a machine can produce x number of products in time t. This calculation does not consider whether the machine is even available at that time or if it is occupied by other orders. There are three different approaches for SNP heuristics:

1. **Multi-level heuristics**
   All set products are considered, including all dependent requirements throughout all locations that affect this product. The *Bills of Material* (BOM) are completely broken down.

2. **Network**
   Only the specified products and all locations related to them in the network are taken into account. Bills of materials are included only on the first level.

3. **Location**
   Planning is done for the specified products and for the specified locations.

Because of the scope of the planning involved, the multi-level SNP heuristic run uses the most resources. Sometimes, by skillfully combining network and location SNP heuristic runs, similar results can be achieved with a better performance.

Capable-to-Match (CTM)

CTM is a finite planning run. This means, for example, that other production orders that currently occupy a machine can also be taken into consideration.

Resources are assumed to have limited availability and calculations are made on the basis of actual availability. Demands are prioritized, and bills of materials are broken down and distributed to the corresponding plants, product by product, until demand is covered.High-priority demands must be covered by production, no matter what. Insufficient capacities can sometimes be tolerated for lower-priority demands. The objective is to find *one* solution to satisfy the planned and concrete demands. Finding the optimal solution is not the objective. As a rule, there are several possibilities for covering planned demand with production.

Assignment between demands and product receipts is called the *pegging structure*. The pegging structure describes the relationship between the receipt elements (production, stock transfer, purchase, and so on) and how they are assigned to sales orders. The process of assigning is called *pegging*. In pegging, bills of materials are completely broken down.

Pegging

Optimizer

Using the SNP optimizer means that the planned and concrete demands are covered by production in such a way that costs are kept as low as possible. This is finite planning. The costs to be taken into account include not only production costs, but also additional costs such as the cost of transport. If there are already sales orders—in other words, if there is concrete demand—then the concrete costs of transporting the product to these customers can be taken into consideration and minimized.

Table 1.1 compares heuristic, CTM, and optimizing. Which method is used depends ultimately on the requirements of the business process. From a technical point of view, SNP optimization is the most resource-intensive method, but because of the extensive calculations, it can be critical to performance.

	Heuristic	CTM	Optimizer
Speed of the SNP run	+++	++	+
Quality of results	+	++	+++
Pegging	–	Pegging possible.	Not relevant because optimal solution is determined.
Parallelization of planning run	+	–	–

Table 1.1 Advantages and disadvantages of different SNP runs

If the planned demand cannot be covered by production, then *deployment* is used. It serves to optimize demand, offer, and distribution capacities. Different criteria such as costs and profit can be taken into consideration. With deployment, for example, the available resources can be redistributed in favor of the production of a particularly sought-after product.

Deployment

The *Transport Load Builder* (TLB) looks after the creation and coordination of transport orders. The objective is to group transport orders in a way that ensures optimal use of the transport available.

The effect of SNP is thus to determine which plant and its production should cover which demands. When the SNP run is complete, the data can be passed on to *Production Planning (PP)/Detailed Scheduling (DS)*.

1.2.3 Production Planning/Detailed Scheduling

All demands (anonymous, sales orders, SNP planned orders) are brought together in the PP/DS module, where planned orders are created and passed on to the linked executing system, such as R/3. With this module, the short-term planning of existing orders can be carried out for one particular plant. The planner bases this on the products and also compares current stock and demands.

Once data is transferred to the PP/DS, the fine planning begins: deciding which planned order is to be carried out in what sequence and on which machine. A planned order is reduced to its individual operations. In planning the individual orders, setup time or offcuts can be optimized, for example.

At the conclusion of the PP/DS, the planning orders can be converted into production orders. The system that executes these production orders is not the APO system, but the external system, such as R/3. Only reduced information on the status of a production order is available in the APO system, and APO "trusts" in the execution of the orders. On delivery completion, the history of the product is deleted from the APO.

Because of the APO system's superordinate role—information on all locations and suppliers is brought together in the APO system—*Global Available-to-Promise* (GATP) is also supported. Dedicated systems such as R/3 can use GATP in APO. Checking rules can also be used with regard to certain locations or product substitutions. If a product is not immediately available, a planned order can also be created for it directly (*Capable-to-Promise*).

Figure 1.2 gives an overview of the planning horizons of the available SCM modules and their planning focus.

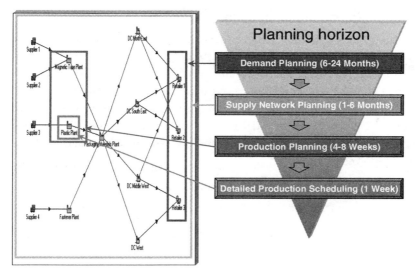

Figure 1.2 Planning horizons and planning areas of the SCM module

During planning in the APO system, the data and properties of these variables are calculated and forecast:

1. Production plants (locations)
2. Transportation routes between locations
3. Products and the different preliminary stages of the products
4. Resources
5. Production process models
6. Necessary production times for a product

At the end of such a planning operation, there is a planning run in which one stage at a time of the planning is codified and the data is passed on to the next step. Due to the complex data volumes to be taken into account, these planning runs use up a lot of resources and are often time-consuming. As a result, as system administrator, you should immediately be informed when these planning runs take place. Administrative maintenance jobs and other jobs that require a lot of system resources should be coordinated with the planning runs so that they do not collide.

You should create a job overview chart in which you record all important jobs—planning runs, in particular—and arrange suitable times for their execution.

1.2.4 Collaborative Planning (CLP)

Because the APO system is the central location for planning and control of production orders, business partners should be allowed a limited view of the information that concerns them. This function is provided by *Collaborative Planning*. To allow business partners to view information, an Internet connection is added to the APO system, and the necessary number of Internet Transaction Servers (ITS) are installed and operated. ITS acts like a gateway between mySAP systems and the Internet. Two main methods are supported:

1. The exchange of data between two APO systems, such as time series

2. Access to authorized data using the Internet Transaction Server

With CLP it is possible to coordinate the planning processes of two business partners by allowing them limited access to planning.

1.3 Technical Conversion

The *Supply Chain Cockpit* (SCC) is the graphic control center for the APO. From here, the user can control all elements of the supply chain. Figure 1.3 shows the components of the SCC.

The cockpit is made up of the following components:

1. **Engineer**
   Maintains a user-defined view of the entire supply chain and models the logistics network.

2. **Cockpit**
   Navigates between locations and integrates different modules. The GPS coordinates are provided for each location, to allow a geographically precise presentation on the world map. The integration of the application modules of APO is actually flowing. The user has an overview of the flow of data between the modules.

3. **Alert monitor**
   Collection point for messages and errors. Serves to support the user. The alert monitor is in no way related to the alert monitor that you know from system administration.
   The alert monitor in SCM supports the user with application-specific messages related to the planning process. This may be in the form of warnings that you have seriously fallen short of the defined minimum stock of a product, for example, or that delivery or production plans cannot be fulfilled in the specified time frame.

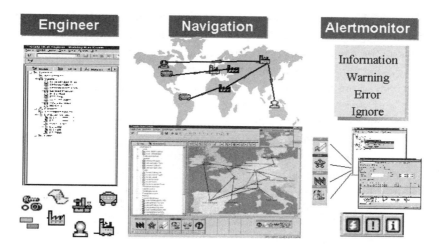

Figure 1.3 APO Supply Chain Cockpit

1.3.1 Data Retention

The basis of the APO is a *data mart*, in which all information needed for Demand Planning is stored and maintained. If the SAP system *Business Information Warehouse* (BW) is used at the same time, the data mart is simultaneously an element of the BW. The modules of the data mart include what are known as *InfoCubes*, as well as product lifecycles, sales forecasts, and advertising strategies.

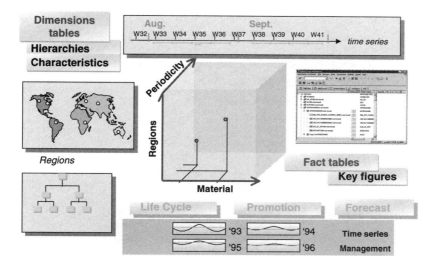

Figure 1.4 The data structure of an InfoCube

The InfoCube as a core element is made up of relational tables linked in a star or snowflake schema. There is a central table (*fact table*), which contains all the characteristics of the InfoCube (see Figure 1.4). By *characteristic* we mean that a feature and its concrete values (such as plant, unit of sale, and so on) are recorded. Characteristics are levels on which you can plan and store data. The *dimension* is stored in the assigned tables. A dimension groups characteristics together by business aspects. For example, sales organization, distribution channel, and region can be grouped together under Sales and Distribution. Furthermore, an amount, in the broadest sense, is stored in the central table of each dimension of an InfoCube. This can be an invoice amount, turnover, stock, sales order value, order quantity, repair time, and so on. These values are the *key figures*.

In addition, each InfoCube is assigned a *period unit* (*time characteristics*). "Period unit" refers to a period of time during which certain InfoCube key figures (*characteristics*) are aggregated, planned, and saved. There can be daily, weekly, monthly, or annual implementations. For both planning with SCM and controlling with BW, queries are made to the database in the form of `key figure according to dimension and time`, and therefore it is necessary to have a list summarizing turnover for each region per month or stock in each plant per week. The following SQL statements arise from this:

```
select sum (turnover) from fact table order by week, plant
```

The key figures are aggregated (`sum`, `avg` etc.) and grouped according to dimension (`order by`) and by the desired periodicity (`order by time unit`).

Figure 1.5 shows an example of a Sales and Distribution InfoCube. This is just an example, however. The structure of a customer's actual InfoCube depends on the actual circumstances.

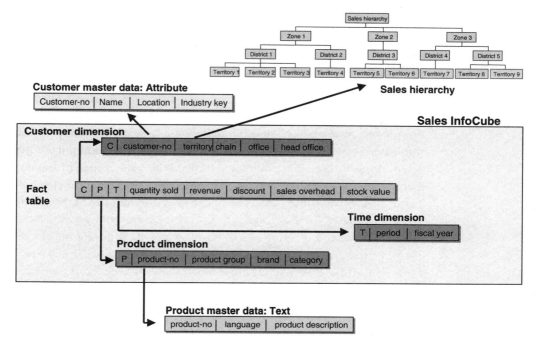

Figure 1.5 Example of the structure of an InfoCube

Circumstances determine the number of tables belonging to an InfoCube and its structure. In Figure 1.5 the fact table is made up of the columns **C, P, T, Quantity Sold, Revenue, Discount, Sales Overhead,** and **Stock Value.** These are the characteristics of the Sales and Distribution InfoCube that are relevant for this particular customer. The *key fields* of the fact table are the dimensions of the InfoCubes. These dimensions in turn have other tables. In our example, the dimensions **C** for **Customer Dimension, P** for **Product Dimension,** and **T** for **Time Dimension** are defined. These three are the basic dimensions created in APO (and also in BW). In real cases, additional dimensions can be defined. In line with the dimensions defined here, there is a **Customer Dimension** table, a **Product Dimension** table, and a **Time Dimension** table. If you take a close look at a record in a fact table, in the field **C** you will see a value that serves as the key to the table **Customer Dimension.** In the **Customer Dimension** table you will find the secondary data on the customer in question. The **Customer Dimension** table is in turn divided into further tables, which contain other customer attributes. For example, it is possible to include a sales hierarchy; large enterprises may wish to divide the sales areas according to territory, which are made up of districts, which are grouped in zones.

In our example, there could also be queries for a list in the following form:

```
Sum of the quantity sold and the stock
for each product
for each customer
for each sales area
for each unit of time
```

From a technical point of view, a multiple join over several tables in the InfoCube is necessary to determine results. You will see that as queries get more complex, more dimensions and further tables are defined in an Info-Cube. Similarly, a growing number of records will have a negative effect on performance. You should therefore try to keep the number of records as low as possible by using aggregation. The choice of time unit for which the key figures are to be recorded can have a particularly strong impact on performance. The time unit should be set to the size you will use in a real business process. It would not make much sense to keep figures for each day, and then use them only in weekly units.

No clients are provided in the APO data mart. The APO system is forcibly not client-able in the way in which you are familiar from R/3. If you need several clients, or, in other words, independent planning instances, you will need a separate APO system for each. However, one R/3 system can supply several APO systems with data and can receive orders from several APO systems.

1.3.2   Data Exchange

In principle it is possible to run an APO system without a direct connection to other SAP or non-SAP systems. The data in the InfoCubes can be recorded manually or transferred at a predefined point in time from, for example, Excel documents. However, you will work most often and most effectively with an active connection between the APO system and other systems. As a result, there is a constant exchange of data between the various systems.

The techniques of the Business Information Warehouse are integrated into APO. This is also apparent in that APO and BW use InfoCubes to implement the central data pool (data mart). Accordingly, an APO system also contains BW controlling functions. However, it is generally advisable to set up a separate Business Information Warehouse; the higher functions of the SAP BW system and the differing system loads make it difficult to optimize a system for both APO and BW requirements. Two separate systems can improve matters.

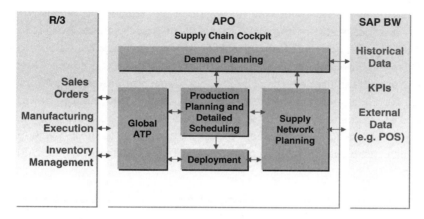

Figure 1.6 Data exchange between systems

An APO system actively exchanges data with R/3 or external systems and, if appropriate, with BW systems (see Figure 1.6). Data flows from the BW system to the DP component and the results are sent back to the BW system. This allows the user to carry out complex analysis of historical data and to create detailed forecasts. The external or R/3 system and the SAP APO system exchange sales orders, the processing of production orders, and inventory management (see Figure 1.7).

Figure 1.7 Data exchange between APO, DP, and BW

1.4   Example of a Business Process

To give you an impression of the complexity of a typical business process in the SCM environment, the following diagrams show the individual steps involved in planning. The starting point for Demand Planning is usually historical statistics from BW systems or other such sources (see Figure 1.8). This data is loaded into the APO system, and usually cleaned up. Once this work has been completed, the forecast run is carried out. Once any possible adjustments have been checked, data is transferred to Supply Network Planning. On the basis of the forecast, the MRP run can be carried out in the R/3 system. If so agreed with suppliers, purchase and plan orders can be done in SNP. These orders are transferred to the R/3 system, which can break down the corresponding bills of materials in the MRP run.

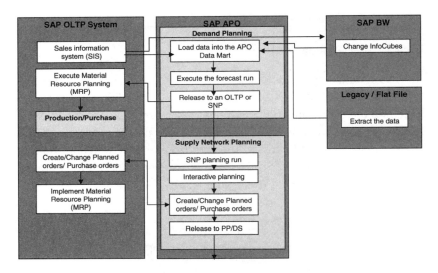

Figure 1.8 Typical operations in Demand Planning and Supply Network Planning

The data can be transferred to PP/DS planning to complete SNP (see Figure 1.9). More detailed planning is carried out in PP/DS. Here, the sequence of production orders can also be determined and optimized with regard to various criteria. In the last step, the confirmed production orders are sent to the R/3 system, where they are processed.

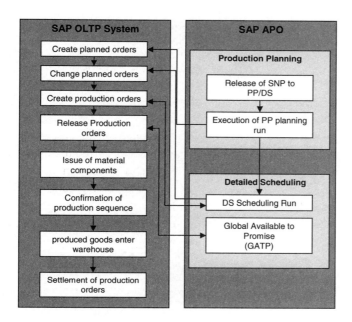

SAP OLTP System

- Create planned orders
- Change planned orders
- Create production orders
- Release Production orders
- Issue of material components
- Confirmation of production sequence
- produced goods enter warehouse
- Settlement of production orders

SAP APO

Production Planning

- Release of SNP to PP/DS
- Execution of PP planning run

Detailed Scheduling

- DS Scheduling Run
- Global Available to Promise (GATP)

Figure 1.9 Planning steps in PP/DS

Building on this business point of view, we will now focus our attention on the technical make-up of SAP's APO system. We will assume that you are sufficiently familiar with the essential features of the architecture of an R/3 system.

2   APO Software

In this chapter we will describe the software components that make up an APO system and the role played by each. What is meant by software maintenance when operating an APO system in connection with an R/3 system?

2.1   The Software Components of APO Systems

The architecture of the APO system can be seen as an extension of the SAP R/3 system. As in the R/3 system, we can differentiate between the presentation, application, and database levels. Because of the similarities of the architecture, the administration tasks involved in running an R/3 system also apply to an APO system. Many tasks can simply be transferred to the APO system as they are.

The SAP GUI is also used for work with the SAP APO system. It has been expanded to include some specific APO functions. This means that additional *Object Component Extension* files (OCX) must be installed.

Front-end

Special additional optimizers have been assigned to the application level of an APO system. These have been incorporated for the necessary optimizing calculations, such as those that result from SNP, Capable-to-Match (CTM), PP/DS, Network Design (ND), Vehicle Scheduling and Routing, and Sequencing.

Optimizer

The various work processes (dialog, spool, background, update, enqueue) are located on the application level, just like in the R/3 system, and they are organized by a dispatcher according to instance. An RDBMS looks after permanent data retention. The software products you already know from the R/3 system (Oracle, SQL Server, Informix, SAP DB, DB/2, etc.) can also be used with this RDMBS. We will henceforth refer to this RDBMS, together with the database, as the *APO DB*.

APO DB

The APO architecture includes some technology that is not used in the R/3 system. For example, the *liveCache* is operated on the database level, apart from the APO DB, in order to meet the demands of SCM. The liveCache, together with the optimizers, represents the main technological difference between R/3 and APO architecture. This expansion of the architecture of the APO system has introduced a series of new and different administration tasks.

liveCache

We will illustrate the problems involved with the help of an example. This example is designed to help you understand the problems of SCM and relational data retention, so marginal conditions have not been included.

One typical concern of SCM is breaking products down into their sub-products and components. Let us say, for example, that you produce computers. In the world of relational data, there would be a table similar to Table 2.1 below.

Product	Component	Quantity	Unit
Pentium 4 PC	case	1	unit
Pentium 4 PC	power pack	1	unit
Pentium 4 PC	mainboard	1	unit
Pentium 4 PC	graphics card	1	unit
Pentium 4 PC	keyboard	1	unit
Pentium 4 PC	mouse	1	unit
Mainboard	Pentium 4 CPU	1	unit
Mainboard	memory	1	unit
PC network	Pentium 4 PC	1	unit
PC network	network card	1	unit
Network card	–	–	–
Pentium 4 CPU	–	–	–
Memory	–	–	–
Graphics card	–	–	–
Keyboard	–	–	–
Mouse	–	–	–
Case	–	–	–
Power pack	–	–	–

Table 2.1 The content and structure of the table "producttab"

Try to generate the complete list of all individual components of a Pentium 4 PC with a single SQL statement. You need to read all lines in the table for which product = 'Pentium 4 PC'. For every value in the field component, the lines for which `product = component` must also be read. The result is as follows:

```
select * from producttab
where product = 'PC Pentium 4' or product in
(select component from producttab where product =
'Pentium 4 PC')
```

The `Mainboard` is made up of two further sub-products, the `Pentium 4` `CPU` and `Memory`. If the sub-products are also broken down, the following command results:

```
select * from producttab where product = 'Pentium 4 PC'
or product in (select component from producttab
   where product = 'Pentium 4 PC')
or product in (select component from producttab
   where product in
       (select component from producttab
       where product = 'Pentium 4 PC'))
```

A command to create a list of all components in a `PC Network` would be even more complex. You need to bear in mind that your product is made up of products, which are in turn made up of products, which are also made up of products, and so on. It will not be possible to formulate a single SQL command for all this. This BOM explosion would lead to a multiple join on the very same table. At this point in the example, we do not wish to discuss all the possible solutions for the maintenance of the relational database. On thing is certain, however: this problem has pushed the relational data model to the limits of its performance ability. In the SCM environment, this type of task is remarkably typical. Products are planned in their entirety, in components and with their attributes. For this reason, object-oriented data retention is inevitable. Because of the complexity of products, the relational approach can never reach the processing speed needed for SCM.

SAP took the step toward the liveCache for this reason. The liveCache is capable of managing object-oriented data structures. To improve performance even further, the objects are fully managed and processed only in the main memory in special object-oriented structures. Only backup copies are written to the hard disk areas; the actual event runs only in the main memory. In principle, the liveCache is a separate database that operates largely in the main memory of a server. As a result, data access times can be greatly improved. The work processes of the APO system, which use the SAP GUI, can use multiple connections (see Figure 2.1). You can decide, based on the application, whether the data should be read or processed by the APO DB or the liveCache.

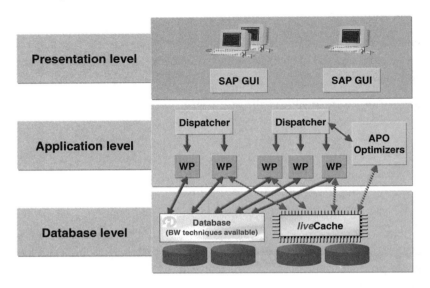

Figure 2.1 Architecture of SAP's APO system

The APO system works with two databases: the APO DB, based on relational database software, and the liveCache, which works mostly in the main memory and supports object-oriented data retention. The liveCache's only task is to improve performance. It achieves this by retaining and processing data in the main memory. The user of the APO system can hardly tell where data is managed and processed. However, for system administration tasks, such as performance analysis, the difference is important.

Data distribution Figure 2.2 gives an impression of how data is distributed between the APO DB and the liveCache. All master data, such as resources, materials, locations, setup matrices, product planning models (PPM), planning tables, transportation routes, and the historical data and forecast data of Demand Planning, is stored in the APO DB. In the liveCache, on the other hand, transaction data necessary for Demand Planning, such as sales and transport orders, purchase orders, including their BOM items, and settings are maintained.

Only the elements in master records that are relevant to planning are loaded in the liveCache. For example, descriptions of materials are not included. Some master data is stored in both the APO DB and in the liveCache. Transaction data is managed only on the liveCache. After installing the APO system, both the APO DB and the liveCache are empty except for administration data. By activating the data transfer from the dedicated systems, data is automatically sent to the APO system; once there, it is automatically divided between the APO DB and the liveCache. You should try to avoid any possible loss of data by selecting a suitable backup strategy. However, if the liveCache is lost, you can use what is referred to as *initialization* of the liveCache to create a new starting point for planning.

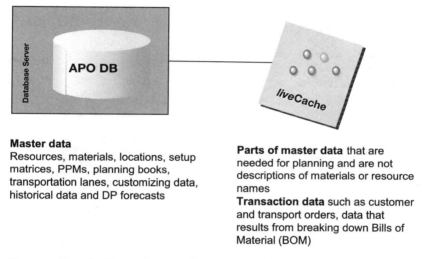

Master data
Resources, materials, locations, setup matrices, PPMs, planning books, transportation lanes, customizing data, historical data and DP forecasts

Parts of master data that are needed for planning and are not descriptions of materials or resource names
Transaction data such as customer and transport orders, data that results from breaking down Bills of Material (BOM)

Figure 2.2 Data distribution between the APO DB and the liveCache

On initialization, the liveCache is completely deleted, then that part of the master data that is relevant to the liveCache is loaded from the APO DB to the liveCache. Because transaction data is stored only in the liveCache, this procedure will not load all relevant transaction data into the liveCache; in order to do that, all the appropriate integration models of the dedicated R/3 systems must be generated and activated again. This means that you have to set up a new initial data load for the transaction data. All other data in the liveCache, such as planning data and planning versions, cannot be reproduced on initialization of the liveCache. As a result, initialization always involves a loss of planning data. Because of this, initialization of the liveCache should be categorically avoided.

Initialization

COM routines *Component-Object-Model* routines (COM routines) are used instead of the SQL interface to increase the speed of data processing. The name *DB procedure* is frequently used instead of the term *COM routine*, but in the future, COM routines will be known as *LCApps*, to reflect the close links to the liveCache and the application logic involved. Although the term has been introduced, the corresponding transactions and documents have not been fully adapted, and we will therefore use the term *COM routine* in this book.

Chapters 4 and 5 describe how the liveCache works and discuss the administration tasks associated with it.

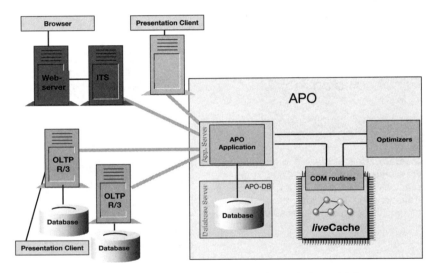

Figure 2.3 System landscape with an APO system and two dedicated R/3 systems

Figure 2.3 shows how a system landscape can be structured when using APO and R/3. In this case, two R/3 systems are connected to the APO system. The APO system is made up of the following components:

► APO DB
► APO instance
► liveCache with COM routines
► Optimizer

If APO collaboration is used, then at least one ITS server will also be used. In order to utilize all of the functions of APO, the above-mentioned special SAP GUI extensions (*OCX packages*) must be installed.

2.2 Scalability

Because of the complexity of APO software, planning the hardware on which an APO system is to be operated is of particular importance. Each component of the APO system makes particular demands that must be taken into account. APO DB and APO instances are similar to R/3, in that the scalability of R/3 instances can be transferred to APO instances.

2.2.1 liveCache with COM Routines

The liveCache with its COM routines forms another, and to a certain extent, independent component of the APO system. The liveCache and COM routines cannot be separated from each other and must always be operated together on one server. Each APO system has one liveCache with COM routines. Much like the APO DB, the liveCache with its COM routines is a central node in the APO system, and operates in the first line of the main memory. Table 2.2 shows the availability of APO software for different hardware and operating systems.

Component	Database software	Operating system
APO DB and application server	DB2/UDB, DB2/390, DB2/400, MS SQL Server, SAP DB, Oracle	AIXm HP-UX, Linux/Intel, Windows NT, OS/390, OS/400, Reliant, Solaris, TRU64 UNIX
liveCache with COM routines	—	Windows NT/Intel, Windows 2000, Solaris, AIX, HP-UX, TRU64 UNIX
Optimizer	—	Windows NT/Intel, Windows 2000

Table 2.2 Availability of the APO components

The 32-bit Windows operating system presents a particular problem. Due to the 32-bit address management, the largest amount of main memory that can be addressed is effectively limited to 2.7 Gb. With the volume of products, locations, and customers that may need to be taken into account during planning, the liveCache can easily grow to more than 3 Gb. Currently, the liveCache can work with up to several hundred Gbs. These demands can be met only by a 64-bit operating system.

PSE36 and AWE In the meantime, software solutions for Windows, such as PSE36 and AWE, are available to cope with this problem. With the help of this software, a 32-bit Windows system can address more than 3 Gb. When you implement the corresponding software, you must also activate the 3 Gb option on the operating system level. This will also allow more than 3 Gb to be used for the data cache of the liveCache. As the size of the data cache increases, however, the performance will be reduced. In addition, further main memory is needed to execute the COM routines. This is called the *OMS Heap* (see Chapter 4), and it is not AWE-compatible. Therefore, this type of memory area cannot be larger than 3 Gb. As a rule of thumb, you can assume that in addition to the data cache, further memory area of around 80% of the size of the data cache will be needed for the OMS Heap. This results in an indirect limitation of the liveCache to around 4 Gb. If, based on the estimation of the liveCache, the data cache size is to be more than 4 Gb, a 64-bit operating system should be selected. This problem with Windows can be solved only by changing to 64-bit addressing. To learn more about this subject, please see the SAPNet Notes 398665 and 384680.

Network In the liveCache, with the aid of COM routines, data is processed and results are returned in a matter of microseconds. As a result, you must have a powerful network connection between the liveCache and the APO instances. It should be at least as strong as that between an APO instance and the APO DB, and should therefore have a bandwidth of around 100 MBits/s.

2.2.2 Optimizer

Optimizers are not absolutely necessary for an APO system. The application determines whether or not optimizers should be used, and if so, which ones. If transport optimizing is not needed, for example, the corresponding optimizer can be omitted. However, if optimization is particularly important, several optimizers of the same type can be used on several servers.

An optimizer is a program based on numeric methods and used to optimize and iterate. The most important requirement of this task is processor performance. In the case of SNP, however, memory-intensive simulations are also carried out. The hardware needed therefore depends on the application profile used. Optimizers communicate very little on the network, in comparison with the liveCache or the APO DB, and are available only for Windows.

2.2.3 Minimum Configuration

The minimum configuration for an APO system consists of a Windows server on which all components are run. Because of the current memory restrictions in Windows systems, the performance of this type of APO system is not sufficient for production operation.

2.2.4 Maximum Configuration

The maximum configuration comprises a server for the APO DB, another for the liveCache with its COM routines, any number of servers with any number of optimizers, and any number of APO instances.

2.2.5 Example of an Average Configuration

Certain key values are a decisive factor in estimating the necessary capacity of an APO system. For a medium-sized system, you should allow for around 20,000 *characteristic combinations*. This refers to the number of products per number of customers per number of locations. If every product is relevant for every customer in every location, the result would be the product of the corresponding amounts—for example, 20 products in 10 locations with 100 customers. Generally, however, only subsets of these need to be taken into account, so the total number of locations, products, and customers can be higher than the number of characteristic combinations used in planning. In addition, the number of key figures in the liveCache is relevant for estimating size. The following values, along with other details, are of particular interest:

▶ Plant-product combinations

▶ Sales orders

▶ Purchase orders

▶ Transport orders

▶ Anonymous demands

▶ Production orders

Let us assume that in the following example all application modules are used in one way or another. In a medium-sized system, for example, we can assume that there would be:

▶ 10 key figures in the liveCache

▶ 20,000 plant-product combinations

▶ 40,000 sales orders

- 20,000 procurement orders
- 20,000 transport orders
- 20,000 anonymous demands
- 10,000 production orders

For background planning runs, a default time frame of one hour is proposed. For this type of system, one server for the APO DB with one APO instance is estimated. The server should have around four to six CPUs, 3 Gb RAM, and 50 Gb hard disk memory. Another server is needed for the liveCache. It should feature two to four CPUs, around 4 Gb RAM, and 50 Gb of hard disk memory. Yet another server should be provided for the optimizer or optimizers, the size of which, again, depends on special key values. This example, however, should not be considered binding. It is only supposed to give you an idea of the sizes involved. What should be clear from this example is the fact that to estimate hardware requirements, you will need fixed assertions for key values of the application. In the above example, only a small portion of these key figures is suggested.

Quicksizing To find out which configuration and which hardware will be most suited to your project, you should use the *Quicksizer*. Quicksizer estimates the hardware requirements you can expect, based on application-specific indicators. With the help of your hardware partner, you can then decide which actual machines best meet these requirements. To run a quicksizing project, you will need to have very detailed information on the planned key values of the application. You should discuss these values with the relevant departments, since they are the ones responsible for making a precise estimate of the necessary parameters. You can find the Qu cksizer on the SAP Web site at *http://www.sap.com* under the name *quicksizer*.

To keep the operating costs of an APO system as low as possible, you should try not to run too many servers. If you have a lot of servers, this means a lot of administration work for each individual server. In addition, the cost of operating the network increases as the number of servers increases.

The network connecting the APO instances and the liveCache, as well as the APO DB, must have a very high capacity. If the liveCache and the APO DB are run on a single server, then this network problem is eliminated. On the other hand, if you operate several components of the APO system on a single server, you should take care that the components do not have a negative effect on the demand for resources. This would lead to reduced performance for the entire APO system.

2.3 Development Landscape

The requirements of the APO environment in regard to the Change & Transport System are similar to those of the R/3 system. Support packages or customer developments should always be tested in a separate development system first. You should therefore run at least two and preferably three APO systems. As with R/3 landscapes, it is recommended that you have a development system, a quality assurance system, and a production system. You should also be aware of the client problem in APO systems, since each APO system can manage only one client in DP.

Copying an APO system to create a system landscape is much more complex than it is for R/3 systems, because ultimately, not only the APO DB but also the liveCache has to be duplicated. Also, an APO system is not a free-standing, independent system; it involves active data exchange with the dedicated systems. In a system copy, these connections must be capped and later re-activated in an appropriate form. Details on copying a complete APO system can be found in SAPNet Note 210564.

To copy an APO system, consistent offline backups of the APO DB and liveCache must first be created. To do this, you need to execute a controlled halt of the liveCache and then of the APO DB. In this way you can ensure that the backups of the APO DB and liveCache to be created match each other. Recoveries for the APO DB and liveCache are then executed on the target machine or machines. Particular attention should be paid to the maintenance of connections in the new APO system. When the copied system is first started, you should ensure that there are no background jobs or other processing taking place which may automatically transfer data to a production system. If there is any possibility that a connection may be made, this should be prevented technically. Data exchange with the original liveCache should also be avoided. In addition, you need to re-establish the connection to the copied liveCache. When the APO DB is copied, the connection data of the original liveCache is transferred.

2.4 Software Maintenance

2.4.1 R/3 Software Maintenance

In order for the APO system to be successfully integrated into and maintained in an existing R/3 landscape, some additional functions must be added to the R/3 system. For this, SAP provides what are known as *plug-ins*, which are essentially transports order that include the necessary programs for realizing the new functions. From a technical point of view, a plug-in is no different from an add-on, such as those available for Industry Solutions (IS).

Add-on technology   The same technology is used in add-ons as in plug-ins. An add-on usually consists of a transport containing new functions and objects, such as programs, tables, and views. To integrate an add-on into a mySAP system, it is often also necessary to make changes to existing objects. An add-on can therefore also imply changes to standard objects in the mySAP system. As a result, as a second step in implementing an add-on, it may be necessary to bring in what is referred to as a *Conflict Resolution Transport* (CRT).

Add-on types   Within add-ons, we can differentiate between add-on packages with and without CRT. Changes to existing objects in the system can be avoided if you use add-on packages without CRT. If numerous customer-specific changes have been made to a system, add-on packages without CRT may be the only feasible option. However, this usually means that certain functions have to be sacrificed, because existing objects cannot and should not be changed.

Add-on technology can be transferred directly to plug-in technology. Here we can also differentiate between modifying and non-modifying plug-ins. The type of plug-in that can be used depends on the R/3 release, the functions required, and the customer-specific modifications. Figure 2.4 suggests possible implementations of plug-ins. The plug-in includes a general interface for connecting an R/3 system to any other mySAP system that is not R/3, such as APO, CRM, or BW.

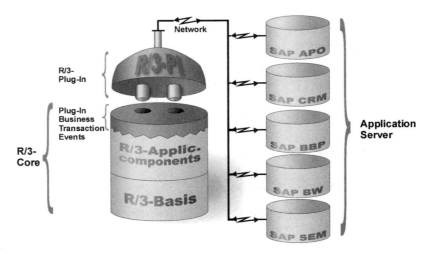

Figure 2.4 Plug-in technology

We can differentiate between a complete plug-in *PI*, which can require CRT, and a partial plug-in *PI-A,* which is CRT-independent. PI-As contain only a subset of the PI of the same version. As a rule, PI-As are non-modifying. Depending on the release of the R/3 system, PIs can be modifying or non-modifying. Table 2.3 gives an overview of which plug-ins can be used for which R/3 release. Further plug-ins are currently being developed.

R/3 release	PI 2000.2, PI 2001.1	PI-A 2000.2, PI-A 2001.1
3.1I	Supported, modifying	Supported, but not for mySAP APO; non-modifying
4.0B	Supported, non-modifying	Supported, but not for mySAP APO; non-modifying
4.5B	Supported, non-modifying	Supported, but not for mySAP APO; non-modifying
4.6B	Supported, non-modifying	Not supported
4.6C	Supported, non-modifying	Not supported

Table 2.3 Overview of plug-ins

PI-As cannot be used to connect an R/3 system to an APO system. To date, PI-As can be used only for communication with mySAP BW, mySAP EBP, and mySAP CRM.

If there is already a PI-A operating in an R/3 system that is to be linked to an APO system, you must first upgrade the PI-A to the PI of the same name. For example, if you are currently using PI-A 2000.2, you must upgrade to PI 2000.2 before you can upgrade to PI 2001.1. Figure 2.5 shows the possible upgrade paths.

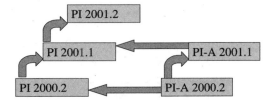

Figure 2.5 Upgrades of PI and PI-A

Installing plug-ins is done in the same way as installing add-ons, using the transaction **SAINT**. As with add-ons, there are also special support packages and upgrades for plug-ins.

If a plug-in is added to an R/3 system, it must also be taken into account when upgrading the R/3 system. When upgrading the R/3 system, you will need the special plug-in upgrade CD. You cannot skip this step.

For further information on plug-ins, see the SAP Web site, and enter *r3-plug-in*.

2.4.2 APO Software Maintenance

APO systems work on the same basis as R/3 systems. As system administrator, you can therefore use the same basic functions you would with an R/3 system. The ABAP programming language and its development tools are also fully supported. Since in an APO system (especially in the DP module), structures and functions from the area of BW are used, an APO system also contains these functions. Therefore, we can say that APO software is made up of R/3 Basis, BW software, and certain APO-specific functions. Table 2.4 shows which releases of these different components lie behind each APO release.

	APO 2.0	APO 3.0	APO 3.1
BW	1.2B	2.0B	2.1C
Basis	4.6A	4.6C	4.6D

Table 2.4 Releases of the components in APO software

APO software contains the full range of functions of a BW system. However, we strongly advise that you not try to resolve BW issues with an APO system. From a technical point of view, BW questions are contrary to SCM tasks. Either optimize your APO system for SCM use, or optimize it for BW. Use a separate BW, distinct from the APO system, for your BW tasks!

 There are patches for all components in the APO system. As you know from the R/3 system, these patches are delivered with *support packages*. Due to the composition of APO systems, support packages for BW, Basis, and ABAP and special support packages for APO may all be of interest to you. In contrast to familiar, existing support packages such as Basis or ABAP support packages, an APO support package can be made up of the following components:

▶ APO kernel
▶ DB interface library
▶ liveCache interface library

- ▶ liveCache software patch
- ▶ COM routines patch
- ▶ Optimizer update
- ▶ Front-end patch (OCX files)

The components contained in each support package are explained in various notes in SAPNet. In general, you will find the support packages in SAPNet under the name *ocs-download.* Read the notes carefully and follow the installation procedure described there. There are often dependencies between components that you must take into account. For example, upgrading the liveCache with its COM routines may require that a certain support package be installed in the APO DB; otherwise, the call interfaces of the COM routines may not correspond with the calls in the report of the APO DB. For urgent corrections, temporary states of individual components can also be made available, outside of support packages. The installation of these patches is described in notes for each case.

2.5 Determining the Version

To find out which support packages have been imported into an R/3 system, select the path **System · Status** from the menu. A list of all support packages relevant for that system will appear. Select **Patches** and you will be shown a list of all support packages imported. This list shows only the transport orders that have been imported during the implementation of a support package, however. Transport naming follows pre-defined conventions. Table 2.5 shows which transport orders are assigned to which modules.

Component	Release	Transport order
SAP_BW	20B	SAPKW20Bxx
SAP BASIS	46C	SAPKB46Cxx
SAP_APO	30A	SAPKY30Axx
SAP_ABA	46C	SAPKA46Cxx

Table 2.5 Naming conventions for transport orders

With APO, however, a support package usually contains other patches to other components, in addition to these transport orders. Each component generally has its own installation routine. Every support package has a note, in which the content and the versions of the individual components are described in detail. For information on dependencies between component releases, see the SAP Web site at *http://service.sap.com/scm* • *mySAP SCM Technology* • *Availability of SPs and COM Builds*.

 You should never implement APO Support Packages only in part, because this will usually lead to error situations.

We will now describe how you can determine the version of the individual components of the liveCache.

2.5.1 APO Kernel

1. Call transaction **SM51**.
2. Select the desired instance.
3. Select **Release information**.

When upgrading the APO kernel, you should make sure that you download the database interface library and the liveCache interface library *dbadaslib* separately and install them from *sapserv<x>* or from the CD. This interface library is necessary for communication with the APO DB and/or with the liveCache. Which database interface library you need depends on the database software used in the APO DB. However, you will always need the liveCache interface *dbadaslib*.

2.5.2 liveCache Kernel

You can determine the liveCache kernel version as follows:

1. Call transaction **LC10**.
2. Select **liveCache: Monitoring** • **Properties**

In the row **liveCache version** you will find information such as KERNEL 7.2.5 BUILD 011-000-217-649. The most important parts are the version of the liveCache, here 7.2.5, and the first part of the BUILD, here 011.

2.5.3 COM Routines

With COM routines, the *change list* lets you know the version. Internally, COM routines are grouped according to the application module. You can find the version of the COM routines by calling transaction **/SAPAPO/OM04** or using the menu path **Tools** • **APO Administration** • **liveCache** • **COM routines** • **Tools** • **COM Version**.

Figure 2.6 gives an example of how the display may look.

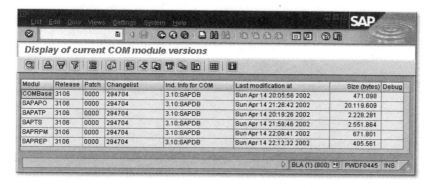

Figure 2.6 Version of the COM routines transaction /SAPAPO/OM04

2.5.4 Optimizer

Several different optimizers can operate with a single APO system. Each optimizer supports only one release.

Call transaction **/SAPAPO/OPT09** or use the menu steps **Tools** • **APO Administration** • **Optimizing** • **Version display**.

2.5.5 SAP GUI

With the further development of the SAP GUI, a portion of the functions is stored on the end user's PC. The graphic preparation of data is undertaken in parts of Object Component Extensions (OCX). For APO, the SAP GUI has had further functions added. As a result, all necessary OCX files must be available in the appropriate version on the front-end PC; otherwise, runtime errors such as CNTL_ERROR may occur. For the end user, these errors appear as problems in the application rather than problems with the local installation. You should check the APO system regularly to see if there are runtime errors caused by problems at the front-end.

There are special patches available for front-ends, about which you can learn in SAPNet notes. You can determine the release of a SAP GUI on the local PC as follows:

1. Start the program SAPLOGON.
2. Click with the right mouse button on the icon on the left, beside the program name in the header line.
3. Select **About SAPGUI**.

Figure 2.7 illustrates the procedure for determining the release.

About...
SAP GUI

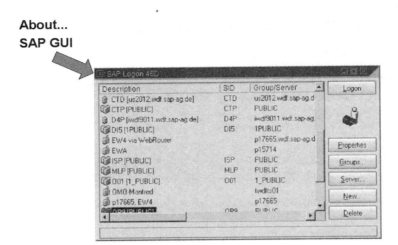

Figure 2.7 Determining the release of the SAP GUI

Figure 2.8 shows the meaning of the individual figures. The ten-digit number in the row **File Version** is decisive in determining the release.

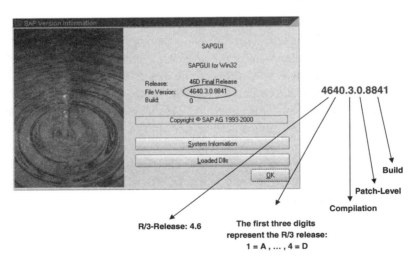

Figure 2.8 The meaning of the figures related to the SAP GUI release

About front-end is also available for displaying the version. The display refers to the corresponding EXE file. However, **About SAPGUI** represents the decisive information for determining the release and for upgrade notes in SAPNet Notes.

2.5.6 qRFC

Among the various software components, qRFC (*queued RFC*) plays a special role. qRFC is used for communication between the APO system and the dedicated systems, such as R/3 (see Chapter 3). The functions of qRFC are included in both R/3 software and APO software as standard functions. However, experience has shown that the functions available are sometimes not sufficient. As a result, qRFC updates and enhancements are often delivered in special subsequent transports. We recommend that you use the latest qRFC release available. Please note that the communicating systems must run the same versions of qRFC.

You can determine the qRFC version as follows:

1. Call transaction **SMQ1**.
2. Select **Execute** or **F8**.
3. From the menu, select **Info · Version**.

You will generally detect a version of type 6.10.43 or higher.

qRFC versions are also partially included in support packages. In some circumstances, when importing a support package, a more up-to-date version of the qRFC may be overwritten. You should check the version of the qRFC before and after upgrading or introducing Basis or APO support packages. If necessary, you should import a newer version of the qRFC.

For APO release 3.0, SAPNet Note 326494 gives an overview of which versions of the components are compatible.

3 The APO System in the System Landscape

This chapter introduces the procedure for integrating the APO system into the R/3 landscape. You will also learn about the tools for managing and monitoring the data transfer interface.

3.1 Basic Principles

Commercial requirements determine how an APO system should be linked to an existing system landscape. The definition of the interface is therefore developed by specialists in the application. The technical implementation and monitoring of this interface, on the other hand, is the work of the systems administrator.

As we have explained above, all master data, such as plant, material, and customer data, is to be sent to the APO system. Transaction data related to this master data is also transferred. This includes sales orders, production orders, warehouse stock, invoices, orders, capacities, and available-to-promise requirements (ATP). For the ATP check, different objects can be transferred, depending on the requirements of the business process. They are managed in the APO system, where they are known as *ATP categories*. The planning is carried out in the APO system on the basis of this data. The results of the planning are sent back to the assigned (dedicated) R/3 systems. These can be, for example, planned orders, procurement orders, ATP results, or production orders.

Since the type and structure of the data related to the data exchange between R/3 and APO systems are known, a standardized interface for data transfer has been developed. This interface is known as the *core interface* (CIF). It is delivered by SAP as an add-on for R/3 systems. Considerations to be taken into account when introducing this type of add-on are detailed in Chapter 2.

SAP provides *Business Application Programming Interfaces* (BAPIs) for linking non-SAP systems to an APO system. BAPIs are standardized procedures that can be used by any number of other applications, taking the defined interfaces into account. SAP provides documentation for all defined BAPIs and guarantees the interface and functions of the BAPI. However, users are responsible for the actual use of the BAPI.

If you try to visualize the integration of the APO system, you will see that first, existing planning-related business objects must be transferred to the APO system. Then both changes to these objects and any additional new objects have to be transferred. All transaction data related to these business objects is relevant to the transfer. Correspondingly, we can distinguish between:

▶ Initial data transfer, which refers to the first-time transfer of a business object

▶ Incremental data transfer, which refers to the transfer of any changes to existing business objects

This applies to both master data such as materials and locations, and transaction data such as sales and production orders.

Global initialization is the very first event in the life-cycle of an APO system. There must be an initial transfer from the dedicated systems of all existing business objects that are relevant to planning. This phase is known as the *initial data loading*. Afterward, other initial data transfers occur whenever new business objects are created. For all transferred objects that already exist in the APO system, the changes and corresponding transaction data must then be transferred. On the other hand, all results of planning in the APO system must automatically flow back into the dedicated systems. In order to guarantee consistency of data in all participating systems, this interface must be reliable, in order to react to disruptions smoothly. Precisely this requirement is guaranteed by the CIF interface. CIF features the following characteristics:

▶ Automatic transfer of the relevant data from the dedicated systems (master and transaction data)

▶ Initial and incremental transfer of master data

▶ Continuous transfer of transaction data

▶ Sending the APO results back to the dedicated systems

▶ Guaranteeing the referential integrity

CIF provides the necessary technology to carry out the connection between the R/3 systems and the APO system. The actual data to be transferred must be defined in Customizing.

Integration model   In the first step, the *integration model* is defined. It includes all the data in an R/3 system that should be transferred to an APO system. The integration model describes how data from an R/3 system is to be presented in an APO system. The following are set:

- Source and target system
- Relevant master data for the initial transfer
- Relevant transaction data for the initial transfer
- The selection and destination of relevant result data, which will be sent back to the R/3 system after planning in the APO system

The simplest way to understand how an integration model works is to imagine a program that is created after the definition. This program is made up of numerous selection commands on the tables, which contain data described by the integration model. When a generated integration model is activated, the program behind it is executed. If new business objects are created, the integration model has to be generated again, so that the selection conditions can be extended to cover the new business objects. After this step comes activation once again—that is to say, the execution of the generated program. With this step, the relevant data is selected and transferred.

The application team is responsible for determining, in accordance with business requirements, how often new business objects should be transferred. A daily transfer of new objects is common. For transferring changes to objects, you can also select between immediate and periodic transfer, depending on the plug-in used. To date, immediate transfer is possible for materials, customers, vendors, classes, and characteristics. Of course, the requirements of the business process are decisive. However, it is recommended that you check these guidelines in detail.

In the APO system, data from the different R/3 systems is grouped together in the *business system group* (BSG). BSG separates the master data from different systems if, for example, different materials have the same material number in different dedicated systems. If the same material numbers are used for the same materials and they can be grouped together, it is not necessary to differentiate using various BSGs. A single shared BSG can be used. Figure 3.1 shows a case in which different BSGs are used to differentiate data. The material number M1 exists in all linked R/3 systems. However, in two systems it refers to a screwdriver, and in a third, to a hammer. These materials cannot be grouped together. Therefore, the logical systems of the R/3 systems must be grouped to different BSGs.

Business System Group

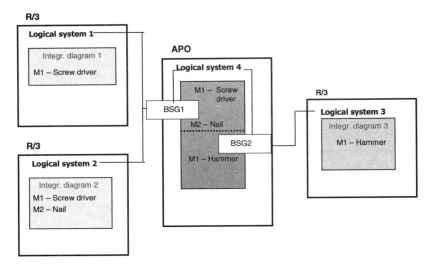

Figure 3.1 Using a Business System Group (BSG)

A shared BSG can be formed only if completely separate number ranges prevent overlapping. Although there may be no overlapping when the system group is defined, it can occur over time if not explicitly excluded by the appropriate customizing. If this cannot be guaranteed, then when several R/3 systems are connected to an APO system it is always necessary to build several BSGs.

3.2   Defining the Business System Group

To prepare an APO system for integration into a system group, the BSG must be defined as described. The following information must be recorded for this:

▶ The logical system name of the BSG

▶ The network connection

▶ The BSG itself

In this way, the APO system knows which systems are going to deliver data and which systems data should be sent to. To give you an overview of how the APO system is integrated into the system landscape, the configuration of the data flow is sketched below. This occurs with the connection of an R/3 system to an APO system.

The first step takes place in the APO system. You should proceed as follows:

1. Select **Tools · Business Engineer · Customizing · SAP Reference IMG · APO Implementation guide · R/3 Basis Customizing · Application Link Enabling (ALE) · Define sender and receiver systems · Setting logical system · Name logical System**. You will receive a list with all known logical systems. A logical system is just the logical name of a system and the client in which data from other systems can be transferred, plus a short description.

2. Define a logical name for the client of your APO system, into which the data from the assigned system should flow. To do this, select **New entries**. The name of the logical system should be formed as in the following sample: `<APO-System name>CLNT<Client number>`.

3. You should then, in accordance with the same sample, gather the system and its clients, which should later transfer data to the defined clients of the APO system.

4. Save your entries.

5. Exit this menu branch and change to the logical system to assign a client. A list of all clients in the APO system appears.

6. Select clients of the APO system relevant to the data transfer. Assign these clients in the **logical system field of the previously recorded name,** `<APO-System name>CLNT<client>`.

7. Save your entry and exit this menu branch.

8. Now change to **systems** in **Configure network · Define target systems for RFC calls**.

9. Select the desired RFC destination.

10. For every previously defined external logical system, record an RFC connection of the same name.

11. Save and test each connection defined.

12. On completion of these steps, the APO system knows the delivering systems assigned to it and can be reached via an RFC connection.

13. In the next step the business unit is built. To do this, exit the menu branch **R/3 Basis Settings**.

14. Change to **Advanced Planner and Optimizer · Basis Settings · Maintain business system group**. A list of all previously defined business system groups appears. A business system group is also no more than a logical name assigned to the APO system and a dedicated system that supplies and receives data. The logical name is thus the name of a connection between the APO system and, for example, an R/3 system.

15. Select **New Entries** to create a new name. The business system group should be named as follows: `<SID of the external system><Client of the external system>`.

16. Save your entry and exit this menu branch.

17. Change to the menu branch **Assign logical system and queue type.** Complete the list of known business system groups byadding those you have just defined. To do this, once again, you select **New entries.** With the queue type you can define whether or not the APO System should work with inbound queues. The consequences of this are described in Section 3.5.

18. Assign the corresponding and previously defined logical system to this new business system group, the external system from which the APO receives data and/or to which it sends data.

19. You should also record the APO system that belongs to the BSG. To make administration easier, you should avoid setting the *R/3 system* flag for the APO system.

20. Save and exit this menu branch.

Work in the APO system is now complete. Preparations must then be carried out in the external system so that data can be exchanged between it and the APO system. Standard R/3 systems must be extended, as described above, to include important functions. This means that the *plug-in* has to be imported. You will find details of the available plug-ins in Chapter 2. All interfaces and techniques in the R/3 system that are needed to exchange data with an APO system are integrated with the plug-in.

3.3 Defining the Integration Model

If the corresponding plug-in is available in the R/3 system, then in the following steps, you must define which data should be transferred to the APO system. The integration models are then created. This includes the following steps:

▶ Defining the logical system

▶ Maintaining the network connections

▶ Selecting the data relevant to planning by defining the integration model

More detailed instructions for creating network connections are as follows:

1. In the first step, the name of the logical system is recorded, so the connection to the APO system is given a logical name. Execute the transaction **SALE** and select **Prepare sender and receiver systems · Set up logical systems · Name logical system**.

2. Enter the name of the logical system for the connection to the APO system, just as you have already defined it in the APO system (`<APO-System name>CLNT<Client of the APO system>`).

3. You must also enter a logical name for the clients of your R/3 system that should send data to the APO system. You have already defined this name in the APO system. It should once again be formed in accordance with the sample `<R/3-System name>CLNT<Client>`.

4. Now change to the menu point **Assign a logical system to a client**. Assign the logical name you have just entered for your R/3 system to the corresponding client.

5. To define the physical connection to the APO system, select **Logistics · Central functions · Supply Chain Management planning interface · Core Interface Advanced Planner and Optimizer · Settings · RFC destinations** (Transaction **SM59**). Apply a connection of type *R/3* to the APO system. The name of the selected connection must be identical to the logical system name of the connection to the APO system (`<APO-System name>CLNT<Client>`).

6. You must identify the R/3 system so that it can be treated as an APO system in the logical system. Record the necessary entry based on the settings via **APO Releases**, where you enter the type of the system (*SAP_APO*) and the release of the APO system.

7. In the menu point **Target system,** define the logical system as the target system. The operation mode is automatically determined from the APO system. The operation session is set at **I** (initial), **T** (activating the delta transfer), or **D** (deactivated), depending on whether, for example, initial datais transferred or the delta for the initial data transfer has been created.

The integration model can now be created. Each integration model describes which data should be transferred between the systems. Thus, you select, for example, the master data or material stocks. The procedure for creating an integration model is described below. Usually, different integration models are created for different business objects, so that several integration models exist.

1. Select **Logistics · Central functions · Supply chain planning interface · Core interface Advanced Planner and Optimizer · Integration model · Generate · Create**.

2. Select an integration model name. In the **Target system** field, assign the previously created logical system names.

3. In the **Application** field, describe which data should be exchanged.

4. A comprehensive list of all data that can be transferred is then made available to you. Select the desired data. The selection possibilities can vary depending on the plug-in used.

5. Save the integration as a variant.

6. Change to the menu point **Activate**.

7. Select the version to be activated or choose the previously saved variant of your integration model by double-clicking on the corresponding row.

8. Activate the integration model with the **Start** button. A popup window will inform you when the activation has been successfully completed.

After successful activation, the initial transfer of data to the connected APO system begins immediately. You can follow the phases of the transfer in the message line of the SAP GUI.

3.3.1 Strategies for Creating the Integration Model

To avoid load peaks when data is being transferred from the R/3 system to the APO system, it is a good idea to define several integration models, rather than relying on a single one. You should, in any case, differentiate between master data and transaction data. You should also make divisions within the master data and transaction data. Ideally, all integration models contain approximately the same physical volume of data. However, you should avoid complex data selection conditions in integration models, because this may lead to a loss of performance when data is being selected.

An integration model is made unique by its name *and* the assigned application. In this way, you can create integration models with identical names for different applications. Should an error occur, it is easier to locate the source of the error, because the error is assigned to an integration model. The "smaller" the integration model is, the smaller the generating data volume and the source of the error.

We recommend that you have about five integration models for transferring master data and five others for transferring transaction data.

As soon as an integration model is generated, the necessary structures and procedures for the transfer are generated in the background. In an R/3 system, however, new data relevant to planning may constantly be created. New master data objects are not automatically adopted into the integration model for transfer. Therefore, you should regularly re-generate and re-activate the integration model. You can do this by regularly running the reports

▶ RIMODGEN for generating
▶ RIMODAC2 for activating

in the background with the corresponding variants for each integration model. The report RIMODINI must run before generating and activating the corresponding integration, in particular, to transfer planning-relevant products, work centers, classes, and characteristics. The report RSPPMCHG works in the same way as the production process model (PPM).

When and how often this type of data transfer is carried out is ultimately decided by the application. This depends on how up-to-date the data set in the APO system needs to be. This information is used to calculate how often the integration model needs to be re-generated and re-activated. Activating an integration model always causes a high load in the dedicated system. The relevant data must be selected and then transferred. Therefore, the load in the APO system is also increased during this action. As system administrator, it is very important that you know when this moment of transfer occurs. You need to take it into account when planning other system activities.

Activating and generating integration models should take place at a time when system load is low.

From a performance point of view, it is advisable to delete obsolete integration models. You can do this by regularly running the report RIMOD-DEL. Only the last two or three integration models of each type should be kept.

3.4 Transferring Incremental Data

When transferring changes to master data, you must decide between immediate or periodical transfer. In theory, you could also completely dispense with the transfer of change data. From an application point of view, however, this is hardly advisable when using the APO system. In order for changes to the master data to be visible in the APO system, you would need a complete new data transfer to the APO system. This initial data load would mean too much effort in terms of time and technology. This method (or lack of method) would make sense only in test systems. For production systems, only immediate or periodic transfer of changes should be used. Once you decide on a method, you must then select the corresponding transfer procedure.

Business trans-action event
The immediate transfer of data is done with *business transaction events* (BTE). In this case, the transfer is triggered at the same time as the change. That is to say, once a change has been carried out to the master data in question, an additional action occurs: the transfer is initiated.

Change pointer
If you select periodic transfer, only a change pointer (*ALE Change Pointer*) is recorded. The actual transfer of data takes place only when the change pointer is analyzed and processed.

For technical and performance-related reasons, the periodic transfer of changes is preferable to transfer using BTEs. Imagine that someone has made a change to master data. Once the data is saved, in the case of a BTE the transfer to the APO system would begin immediately. Soon afterward, however, the person notices that there is a mistake in the change. The master data must be changed once again. This change also triggers an immediate transfer to the APO system. From this example we can see that if BTEs are used, data transfers take place much more frequently than with the periodic transfer of changes. This can cause problems with workload, particularly in the case of mass changes.

 It is important that you discuss whether an immediate data transfer is actually necessary for the application. You should try to keep the number of transfers of change data as low as possible. Change data should be transferred when the system load is low.

Coordinate the change transfer with the generation and activation of integration models. Change transfers marked with a change pointer are analyzed and transferred when an integration model is being generated and activated. Therefore, it is not necessary to have a change transfer in direct connection with the new creation of an integration model.

Customizing the transfer of incremental data occurs in the following steps in the R/3 system:

1. Execute transaction **CFC5**.

2. Select the desired transfer method:

   ▶ **No incremental transfer**
   Changes are not transferred. The APO system can be updated only if a complete initial data load is carried out from time to time. As a result, this method is somewhat irrelevant for production operation.

   ▶ **Business Transaction Event**
   This method is resource-intensive. No further actions are necessary.

   ▶ **ALE Change Pointer**
   If you select this method, then steps 3 to 7 are necessary.

3. Start the transaction **SALE · Application Link Enabling (ALE) · Modeling and implementing business processes · Configure distribution of master data · Arrange replication of changed data · General activation of change pointers** (transaction **BD61**).

4. Activate the **Change Pointers according to message type** (transaction **BD50**).

5. In newer plug-ins, the message type relevant to data transfer is automatically selected by the system. If this does not occur, mark the message types. The message types relevant to CIF comply with naming conventions; they all start with "CIF". The message types available include CIFMAT, for materials, CIFVEN, for vendors, CIFCUS, for customer data, and CIFSRC, for info records. There can also be CIFPPM for BOMs (Bills of Material) and routings, depending on the support package. Selecting the correct message type is the task of the relevant department. Therefore, we will not go into further details here.

6. Save the settings as a variant of the report RCPTRAN4.

7. You should schedule this variant of the report for background processing in the preferred period for data transfer.

Data transfer can also be initiated manually using transaction **CFP1**. For production operation, however, this is undesirable.

For reasons of performance, obsolete, processed change pointers should regularly be deleted. Use the report RBDCPCLR to do this. It is recommended that you delete all obsolete change pointers that are more than two weeks old.

Table 3.1 shows all reports that are regularly used in a dedicated R/3 system for transferring data to an APO system. Basis and the relevant departments should work in close collaboration to decide when and how often these background jobs should be run.

Report	Meaning	Transaction
RIMODGEN	Generating integration models	CFM1
RIMODAC2	Activating integration models	CFM2
RIMODINI	Initialization of the transfer of plannable products, work centers, classes, and characteristics	
RSPPMCHG	Initialization of the transfer of production process models (PPM)	
RIMODDEL	Deleting obsolete integration models	CFM7
RCPTRAN4	Incremental data transfer of master data	CFP1
RBDCPCLR	Deleting obsolete change pointers	BD22

Table 3.1 Overview of reports for data transfer in the R/3 system

Please note that when scheduling the reports, RIMODGEN should be run first, then RIMODAC2. In this way, the "old" integration model is seamlessly displaced by the "new" one. What actually happens is the initial transfer of the newly added business objects. This method of procedure is known as *delta logic*. If, on the other hand, you deactivate the "old" integration model explicitly and then activate it again, not only is the newly added delta volume transferred, but all business objects are also transferred again. This corresponds to a complete new initial data transfer.

3.5 The Technical Basis of the Core Interface (CIF)

The technical implementation of the CIF is based on qRFC (*queued Remote Function Call*). RFC is based on CPI-C technology and supports the call and execution of remote function modules, such as those in SAP systems. If a business object is transferred from one system to another, the object is deconstructed into its component parts. The individual *requests* are placed in transfer queues (*outbound queues*). The individual requests are collected from there and placed in the corresponding processing queue (*inbound queues*) in the target system. The inbound queues are processed by the target system. Alternatively, you can choose not to use inbound queues.

In this case, the requests entering the target system are processed immediately on arrival. The sending system waits until the processing is complete.

Any number of outbound queues can be created in the R/3 system (source system). Each queue has a unique name, which refers to the objects it contains. Objects of the same type are assigned to a *channel*. The name of the channel is made up of the two characters "CF", followed by the business object type. Table 3.2 shows which channels are used for which objects in the APO environment.

Business objects	Channel
Initial supply	CF_ADC_LOAD
Stock	CFSTK
Orders and Preqs	CFPO
Planned orders/production orders	CFPLO
Sales orders	CFSLS
Manual reservations	CFRSV
Confirmations	CFCNF
Planned independent requirements	CFPIR
Requirements reduction of PIR	CFMAT
Production campaigns	CFPCM
Master data: Classes	CFCLA
Master data: Characteristics	CFCHR
Shipments	CFSHP
Planning tables	CFCUVT

Table 3.2 Channels for data transfer in R/3 systems

The corresponding queue name is formed by adding the document number to the channel name.

In the APO system, similar rules are used for forming channel names. The first two items in the channel are also "CF", which is short for CIF. The following two items indicate the object type. To form the queue names, the channel names are extended by a further four items, which represent the cross total of the order number. If there is an extremely high number of send requests from the APO system to the R/3 systems, there may be overlapping in the four-figure cross totals of the order number. In this case you can use the 20-digit queue names (see SAPNet Note 440735).

qRFC technology is used not only in the APO environment; it is also used with mySAP CRM software, for example. Allocating to the different queues is very clear thanks to the naming convention.

When, how many, and which queues should be created is set in the program and cannot be influenced from outside. Figure 3.2 shows how the sub-objects of a business object can be distributed over the different queues. All sub-objects of a business object are processed as a *logical unit of work* (LUW), because the sub-objects are logically linked.

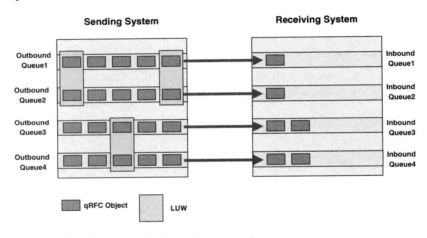

Figure 3.2 Distribution of a business object over the queue

Within a queue, the sequence constancy holds. This is necessary because the business objects to be transferred may be linked to each other. Each individual queue is processed or transferred according to the FIFO principle (*first in, first out*). Each outbound queue has a counterpart inbound queue in the target system. Outbound queues are formed in the local system for the data that needs to be sent. Inbound queues contain the objects that have been transferred from one system and are waiting to be processed in the local system. The qRFC uses transactional RFCs (tRFC) to transfer the data, which means that the ACID principles, familiar from transactions, are applied to tRFC "("ACID" stands for Atomic, Consistent, Isolation, Durable). Once the objects are fully transferred to the corresponding inbound queue in the target system, processing can begin there. If an error occurs during the processing of a sub-object in an LUW, the corresponding queue is paused. All requests coming after it in the queue have to wait for the problem to be solved and the queue to start again. Since all objects in an LUW are logically linked, all other queues containing sub-objects of the defective LUW must also be paused. According to the transaction principles, LUWs are processed either completely, or not at all. Because of the dependencies between the sub-objects, in the worst case, any number of queues can be brought to a standstill. The data transfer may be extremely limited, or may completely break down.

3.5.1 Technical Conversion and Consequences

qRFC technology is a standard technology which, as we have mentioned above, is also used for other purposes than transferring data between the APO system and R/3 systems. When used between APO and R/3 systems, however, some particular features come into effect.

With Inbound Queues

It is not strictly necessary to use inbound queues when data is being transferred. For APO release 3.0, the use of inbound queues was made possible only with the introduction of APO Support Package 14. For R/3, plug-in 2001.1 or higher is also needed. You have to set whether the connection is to be processed with or without inbound queues. In the standard configuration, APO and R/3 software is delivered without the use of inbound queues. To activate inbound queues in the R/3 system (except for initial data supply), proceed as follows:

1. Start table maintenance in the R/3 source system, using transaction **SE16**.
2. Select the table **CIFOPMODE**. You will find an entry for each source client and its related logical target system.
3. In the column **QUEUETYPE,** enter the value I for the desired clients and the target system, **to activate usage of inbound queues.**

Inbound queues are processed in the target system using an inbound scheduler. To put it another way, in a defined time interval all queues registered in the scheduler will be checked for new requests and processed. MAXTIME defines how long the scheduler should spend processing each one. With the help of this parameter, you can regulate the load on the system caused by processing inbound queues. The lower the MAXTIME, the lower the load, but the longer the processing time for a certain volume of requests in the queue. In addition, you can set how often processing should be re-tried should problems occur (NRETRY). The interval between two attempts is determined by the parameter TDELAY. With the help of the USERDEST parameter, you can specify users and clients that can process a recorded queue. To this end, a connection is assigned to the parameter USERDEST. The connection data is recorded with transaction **SM59**.

If there are logon groups or server groups defined in your system, you can also use this load distribution for processing inbound queues. In this case, use parameter USERDEST to define the server group that should be used for processing. To register queues, proceed as follows:

1. Start transaction **SMQR** in the target system.

2. Select the **Registration** button. Figure 3.3 shows the screen in which the parameters described can be maintained.

3. Enter CF* as the queue name, to register all APO inbound queues.

4. Maintain all other parameters. Figure 3.3 shows a common configuration. The inbound queues are processed for a maximum of sixty seconds each (MAXTIME). If problems occur, the processing is re-tried a maximum of 30 times (NRETRY) with a pause of 300 seconds between each attempt (TDELAY). No particular logon group has been defined for processing.

5. Save the settings.

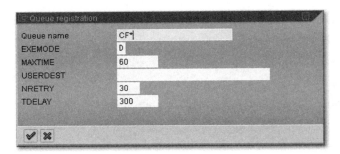

Figure 3.3 Registering inbound queues

After registration you will see an image in the inbound scheduler more or less like that shown in Figure 3.4.

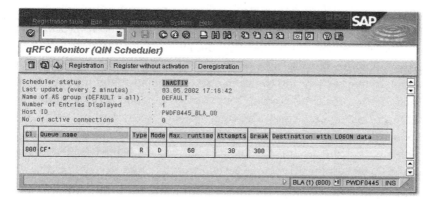

Figure 3.4 Inbound scheduler with registered queues (transaction SMQR)

The current scheduler status is displayed in the row of the same name. The line **Last Update** shows you when the scheduler was last activated and when queues were processed.

You can use **Edit · Change AS group** to assign a selected server group or logon group to all registered queues. Be careful to check that the logon group you select actually exists (transaction **RZ12**). **Name of the AS group: DEFAULT** means that all instances and their dialog work processes are used for processing the inbound queues.

Registering queues is always done according to client. If you send to more than one client in the target system, you must register the queue in each client in the target system.

You must execute this configuration step in both the APO and each dedicated R/3 system, since each system is simultaneously a sending and a receiving system. Basically, it is better to transfer with inbound queues than without.

Without Inbound Queues

If inbound queues are not used, requests are sent directly from the outbound queue to the target system, where they must be processed immediately. The requests are processed with the help of dialog work processes. As a result, the receiving system can overload if too many requests come in. This occurs if there are not enough dialog work processes available for the dialog users and the incoming queries. Inbound queues would protect against such an overload. In principle, they act like a temporary buffer. In the first step, the target system would only transfer the data to the inbound queues of the target system, which would then process the requests. Again, dialog work processes would be needed to process the requests in the inbound queues. Without inbound queues, the source system would have to wait for the successful processing of its requests in the target system. As a result, the source system would spend more time on each request. If a system group runs without inbound queues, problems with processing requests in the target system lead to crashes in the outbound queues in the source system! If, on the other hand, you are working with inbound queues, there would be a termination in the inbound queue of the target system. The source system would not be affected by this. As a result, for large transfer loads, it is better to operate a system group with inbound queues than without. Basically, inbound queues form a temporary buffer for incoming processing requests.

If there are no inbound queues, overload situations in the target system have repercussions in the outbound queues in the source system, such as Cpicerr. Dialog users of the target system will complain of very slow performance. For this reason, we recommend that you limit the number of incoming requests allowed. Table 3.3 shows the instance profile parameters available for this.

Profile parameter	Meaning	Default value	Recommended
gw/max_conn	Maximum number of connections allowed for a gateway of an instance	20	1,000 (if necessary, can be increased to 2,000)
gw/max_overflow_size	Maximum swap space for CPIC requests at gateway for Basis R/3 >= 4.6D	–	25,000,000
gw/max_shm_req	Maximum number of CPIC requests to gateway for Basis R/3 < 4.6D	–	400
rdisp/max_comm_entries	Maximum number of connections that can be open in an application server	100	2,000
rdisp/rfc_max_comm_ entries	Maximum number of RFC connections allowed, in relation to disp/max_comm_entries, in percent	90	

Table 3.3 Important profile parameters for the configuration of RFC connections

Profile parameter	Meaning	Default value	Recommended
rdisp/rfc_max_own_used_wp	Maximum number of dialog processes allowed as a percentage of the total number occupied by qRFC requests	75	
rdisp/rfc_min_wait_ dia_wp	The number of work processes kept free, that is, not to be used for sending qRFC requests	1	Less than the total number of dialog work processes; at least 5
rdisp/tm_max_no	Maximum number of connections to an instance	–	2,000

Table 3.3 Important profile parameters for the configuration of RFC connections (continued)

You will find further details for working with inbound queues in SAPNet Notes 13757, 74141, 384971 and 384077.

You should try to estimate the load that will occur from incoming requests in both the APO system and the dedicated R/3 systems as accurately as possible. To do so, you will need to work in close collaboration with the relevant departments, who can inform you of the frequency of changes to data in the R/3 systems that are relevant to the APO system. The specialist APO departments must also be able to provide information on their activities.

You should limit the maximum number of dialog work processes that can be occupied by qRFCs. To ensure that the load caused by qRFCs affects the actual dialog mode as little as possible, the use of a separate application server or an instance has also proven valuable. If the instance is used only for integration purposes, it can be specially configured for this. As a result, there is less danger of interfering with the work of actual dialog users.

Outbound Scheduler

With qRFC release 6.10.42 (see Chapter 2) a scheduler is also provided for processing the outbound queue. In older releases of qRFC, requests in the outbound queue are processed on the spot, using all available resources. If there are too many outbound queues, this can lead to an overload situation in the source system. If the same large number of requests is sent to the target system, this can also bring about an overload situation there, especially if it is working without inbound queues. If the target system cannot react quickly enough, this will result in crashes in the source system. With the outbound scheduler you can adapt the processing of outbound queues to your requirements.

Concerning configuration and functions, the outbound scheduler is the same as the inbound scheduler. Use transaction **SMQS** to configure the outbound scheduler. As you already know, first the queues relevant to the outbound scheduler must be registered according to client. You can do this using the **Registration** button. Registration is done not according to queue, however, but according to logical destination (parameter DESTINATION). You can use the parameter MAXCONN to limit the number of dialog work processes used in the local system to process the requests. In this way you also limit the maximum number of connections in the target system. To find the best possible value for this parameter, you must consider the total number of dialog work processes available in the source system and in the target system. Even at full load, there should always be enough dialog work processes for the dialog users. The parameter MAXTIME determines the maximum length of time the scheduler should spend processing one outbound queue in one run. This means that you can limit the load caused by processing the outbound queue in both the source system and the target system. This is one clear advantage of the outbound scheduler. Figure 3.5 shows how an outbound queue is registered to the logical destination APOCLNT800. The maximum number of dialog work processes to be used is limited to ten (MAXCONN). A maximum of two seconds should be spent processing each one (MAXTIME).

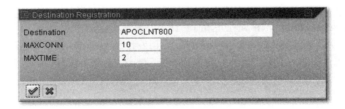

Figure 3.5 Registration of outbound queues

The initial screen of the outbound scheduler (transaction **SMQS**) displays all queues in the form of a table (see Figure 3.6). The value in the column **Type** lets you know if queues are registered for a destination (value R) or not (value U). The settings for the parameter MAXCONN can be read in the column **Max. conn**, and for the parameter MAXTIME, in the column **Max-**

time in seconds in the registration table. In the **Status** column, INACTIVE shows that there are currently no requests in the queue being processed for this destination. Once the scheduler starts processing, the status for a destination changes to ACTIVE.

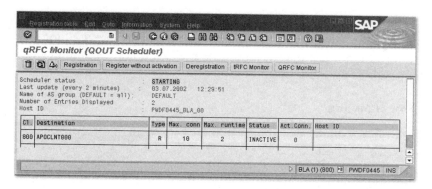

Figure 3.6 Outbound scheduler

It is also possible to determine the status of the scheduler itself. It is displayed in the row **Scheduler Status**, with the following meaning:

▶ INACTIVE
Not active.

▶ STARTING
Just starting to process.

▶ ACTIVE
Processing.

▶ WAITING
Waiting for available dialog work processes in the source system. This status indicates a bottleneck in the sending system, caused because there are not enough dialog work processes available for processing, at least for the moment. If you notice this status frequently, you should either reduce the number of dialog work processes that can be used for processing (Parameter MAXCONN) or check to see if the number of available dialog work processes in the system can be increased.

▶ SYSFAIL
A system error (runtime error) occurred when processing at least one queue. If you are working without inbound queues in the target system, you will most likely see that the error has occurred in the target

system. If you are using inbound queues, however, the error probably occurred in the local system when processing the outbound queue.

▶ CPICFAIL
An error occurred when connecting to the target system.

As with the inbound scheduler, you can also define logon groups for the outbound scheduler (**Edit · Change AS group**), which are used for processing. DEFAULT also indicates here that all instances in the source system are used for processing.

Error Handling

Since qRFC requests are handled with the help of tRFC, tRFC options can also have an effect on the qRFC transmissions. Admittedly, this depends on the qRFC version used. A tRFC connection can be configured in such a way that if there is a problem with transmission, a background job is automatically scheduled to try the transmission again after a defined period of time. You can also define the number of transmission attempts. For qRFC versions earlier than 6.20.043, this technique is also used for connection problems in the qRFC environment. You can use transaction **SM59** to help you make the necessary settings. Select **Destination · TRFC options** to view the possible customizing settings. The delay between attempts should be between two and three minutes, and the number of transfer attempts should be set at around 30, but the exact configuration must be optimized by observation. This technique has already proven to be critical in systems with a very high number of transmission requests and a sudden problem with connection. In extreme situations this automatic scheduling can actually cause overload situations in the sending system. The automatically generated background job is based on the report RSARFCEX. Alternatively, you may decide to ignore the automatic scheduling of this type of job. The report RSARFCEX can periodically be scheduled manually. Which of the procedures described is best for each customer situation cannot be determined globally. To date, most configurations have used automatic scheduling of the background job.

Since qRFC version 6.20.043, this technique has been broken down into two new reports, which are specially suited to qRFC requirements. If there is a termination of the outbound queue, another processing attempt can be made with the help of report RSQOWKEX. Blocked requests in inbound queues can automatically be tackled again using RSQIWKEX. For this, you should schedule the reports RSQOWKEX and RSQIWKEX as regular background jobs. We recommend a frequency of around 30 minutes. With this, requests that have been stopped due to network problems are re-processed, as are those that have been stopped for other technical reasons, such as runtime errors or authorization problems. Terminations of the type *sysload* in outbound queues are an exception, since these are caused by overload situations in the sending system. Overload means that not enough dialog work processes are available in the sending system to process the queue requirements. In this case, the processing strategy is usually changed. The queued requests are no longer sent in parallel from several work processes; instead, they are sent sequentially from a single one. As a result, the load on the target system is substantially reduced.

Alternatively, terminations due to overload can be dealt with using automatically generated background jobs. For this, the instance parameter `abap/trfc_old_sysload` must be set to the value 1. If an overload situation occurs in the sending system, a special background job is automatically scheduled to process again. The name of the background job is formed as follows: `ARFC:SYSLOAD1<Client><User>`. The scheduled report is `RSTRFCSL`. Because a single background job is generated for each breakdown of a request, serious overload problems in the source system can quickly lead to a high number of such jobs. This has a negative effect on the source system. In this case it is also difficult to decide on the best way to proceed. For further information, see SAPNet Notes 437718 and 442478 as well as notes for the currently available versions of qRFC.

3.6   Monitoring the qRFC Queue

Monitoring the queue is one of the key tasks of the APO system administrator. Unlike the core R/3 systems, handling problems of the qRFC queue often requires application-specific know-how, and therefore collaboration between APO system administration and the relevant departments is obligatory. You should also take the role of the integration administrator into account. The strong flow of information between the R/3, APO, any external systems, and other SAP systems requires a comprehensive, all-encompassing view of the system landscape and its problems. Errors during data exchange can be identified only through regular monitoring of the systems.

3.6.1   qRFC Alert Monitor

In APO systems you maintain special alert monitors for queues. The `/SAPAPO/RCIFQUEUECHECK` report is for monitoring outbound queues and `/SAPAPO/RCIFINQUEUECHECK` is for monitoring inbound queues.

Both reports should be processed as background jobs in the APO system at intervals of around 15 minutes. You should simultaneously analyze the queues in the APO system and those in any remote R/3 system. If several R/3 systems are linked to the APO system, a variant of the corresponding report must be created and scheduled for each R/3 system.

Scheduling the jobs is done with transaction **SM36**, as you know from R/3 systems. First, you must create a variant of the report. To do so, you can use the APAB Editor (transaction **SE38**), for example. The selection screen of the report allows you to specify target system and source system according to queue. In the event of an error, according to the selection, a message can be sent to a selected group of people, in a form such as e-mail. Using the qRFC alert monitor is the easiest way to obtain information about any problems that occur. Fast reaction to any errors that occur is particularly important in qRFC. Again, you should fully appreciate the fact that the sequential processing of the queue is absolutely necessary, due to the way in which the applications are related. For example, if the creation of a material fails, a subsequent request that perhaps needs to access precisely this material cannot be moved forward. As a result, the entire processing of a queue grinds to a halt when the object waiting to be processed cannot be dealt with. Working through the queue can be continued only after the problem has been eliminated.

Deleting individual objects in a queue will inevitably leads to inconsistencies between the datasets of the systems, and should be avoided at all costs.

3.6.2 SCM Queue Manager

The SCM Queue Manager allows for cross-system monitoring of queues generated as a result of using CIF. It is suitable for use with both inbound and outbound queues.

The SCM Queue Manager was delivered subsequently with support packages, first only for outbound queues and later for inbound queues as well. See SAPNet Notes 460538, 434888, 419178, and 460537. You can start the SCM Queue Manager using **/SAPAPO/CQ** (report `/SAPAPO/RCIF-QUEUECTRL`).

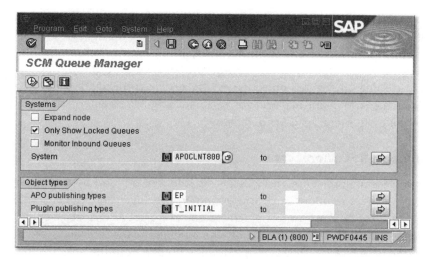

Figure 3.7 Entry to the SCM Queue Manager

In the initial screen, the display can be limited to selected logical systems and to object types (see Figure 3.7). For reasons of performance, if there is a large number of queues, the option **Expand nodes** should not be used. As a result, the SCM Queue Manager displays the queues belonging to a system only if they are needed and selected directly. By *object types* we mean the objects transferred from the system view in each case. Table 3.4 shows the object types visible in the APO and R/3 systems, respectively.

APO system	R/3 system
External procurement	Initial supply
In-house production	Purchase orders
Planned independent requirements	Planned/production orders
Production campaigns	Sales orders
Shipments	Production campaigns
Deliveries	Confirmations
Confirmations	Shipments
Confirmations on deletion (Automotive area)	Stocks
Reporting point (Automotive area)	Characteristics
Reservations	Classes

Table 3.4 Object types in CIF

In contrast to the monitors described below, the SCM queue monitor gives an application-oriented view of the queues of an object type, which is of particular interest for the heads of departments. Icons are used to display the status of the queues from the point of view of object types. Double-clicking on selected object types displays the corresponding queues. From the SCM queue manager you can branch to the rather technical view of the qRFC monitors described below.

3.6.3   qRFC Monitors

qRFC technology is not an APO-specific solution. It is also used in other SAP software solutions, such as CRM, Enterprise Buyer, and Mobile Sales, and as a result, the monitors described below are not APO-specific either. These monitors are available in both the sending and the receiving system. In the case of APO, they can therefore be used in both the assigned R/3 systems and the APO system.

Outbound Queues

Transaction **SMQ1** is used for detailed error analysis, as a tool for information on status, and for managing outbound queues. The underlying monitor is equally available in R/3 and APO systems. Because queues in a system are operated depending on the client, the display can be limited to selected clients in the initial screen of the outbound queue monitor. First, all queues created are displayed in the local system. Each queue is identified by a name. In the APO environment these names always begin with "CF". The following two characters give further information on the application in question (see also Table 3.2). By double-clicking on individual queues or by checking selected queues, the view can be limited to these queues. In the following list a range of functions is available with icons.

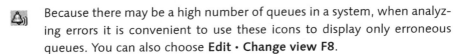

Because there may be a high number of queues in a system, when analyzing errors it is convenient to use these icons to display only erroneous queues. You can also choose **Edit · Change view F8**.

By double-clicking on the desired queue all objects in this queue are displayed with their processing status. You can also get further information on a selected object by double-clicking on the object.

This function allows the immediate activation of qRFC processing. The selected outbound queue's requests are immediately sent to the target system.

A stop mark is set at the end of the selected outbound queue. All requests before this are processed. Once the stop mark is reached, the queue automatically stops. You can repeat this function to place any number of stop marks in a queue. This can be used for targeted testing of transmissions, for example.

In contrast, by immediately locking, the queue is paused on the spot. Only the request currently being processed is interrupted and rolled back. In the case of a processing procedure that runs over a longer period of time, this can be used for error analysis.

The first stop mark in the selected queues is removed. The qRFC manager is immediately started, in order to begin processing. If there are further stop marks in a queue, the queue automatically pauses at the next stop mark.

With this function, only the first stop mark is removed. However, processing does not begin again just yet. It must be started again in a separate action.

By double-clicking on the individual outbound queue, you reach a list of all requests in the selected queue. All columns displayed and their meaning are summarized in Table 3.5.

Column	Role
Clt	Client to which the queue is assigned
User	User under which the queue is being processed
Function module	Function module called in the target system for processing
Queue name	Name of the queue in which the request is located
Destination	Logical system name of the target system
Date	Date on which the request was placed in the queue
Time	Time at which the request was placed in the queue
Status text	Error text, should processing fail
TID	Transaction ID: An internal identifier is assigned to each request entering the queue. The request can be traced in the system using this transaction ID.
Host	Name of the application server on which the request was created

Table 3.5 Meaning of the columns in the queue display

Column	Role
Tktn	Transaction from which the request originates in the source system
Program	Program that created the request in the source system
Rept	Processing attempt number for this request

Table 3.5 Meaning of the columns in the queue display (continued)

By double-clicking on the column of a selected request in the queue again, the details on the request corresponding to this column are displayed.

Interrupting the Entire Data Transfer

It is sometimes necessary to completely interrupt the data transfer into or out of a certain system in the system group. One reason for this is that an upgrade or a recovery may be pending. Essentially, the outbound scheduler reacts to the fact that the target system is unavailable and the data transfer is attempted again and again before a positive interruption occurs. These repeated attempts create unnecessary load for the source system, something that can be avoided by planned maintenance measures to coordinate a pause in the queue. Queues can be stopped immediately, or a stop mark can be inserted at the end of the queue. If there is an immediate pause, transfers that have already started are interrupted and rolled back, and the status is set to **Stop**. If the receiving system is not able to receive, this is the appropriate method for stopping the queues. To pause all outbound queues or selected queues, you can proceed as follows:

1. Call transaction **SMQ1**.
2. Display all queues with a target system (*Queue Destination*) that should be excluded from data transfer.
3. Select any queue.
4. From the menu select **Edit · Generic queue · Lock or Immediate lock**. You can also use the corresponding icons.
5. Enter the desired queue and the corresponding target system. Queues from the APO environment always begin with "CF". With the help of the generic entry "CF"*", all APO-related outbound queues are stopped.

You can monitor the status of individual outbound queues in the queue overview of transaction **SMQ1**. If queues are paused in the mode **Immediate lock**, then their status will change to **Stop** at the next processing attempt by the scheduler. If, on the other hand, a queue with the mode **Lock** is paused, it does not change to the **Stop** mode until the stop mark has been reached.

Locking queues with the help of the report program RSTRFCQ1 is easier. This report supports three parameters. In addition to the queue name, which can, again, be generic, the destination (logical system name) is also requested. By checking the parameter FORCE, selected queues can be paused immediately. This corresponds to the **Immediate lock** function from the menu of transaction **SMQ1**. Thanks to transaction consistency, this does not result in inconsistencies. When the queue is started again, the objects are transferred once more.

To re-activate outbound queues after a pause or after eliminating an error, you can once again use the menu functions of transaction **SMQ1** or a report program. This report program is called RSTRFCQ3, and it makes four parameters available. Once again, you have to enter the queue name, which can be generic, and the target system. In addition, when starting the outbound queues again you can decide to start them with or without activation (parameter NO_ACT). If you choose not to activate, only the stop mark is removed. Processing starts again only when the outbound scheduler is next started. In addition, report RSTRFCQ3 offers a FORCE parameter. If this parameter is not set, report RSTRFCQ3 removes all stop marks and, where appropriate, starts processing the queues. If many queues are paused or stopped because of errors, there are dependencies between the queues. If, due to such dependencies, a queue cannot be processed in the first attempt, its status automatically changes to **Stop** again. For this reason the report program must be run several times to restart all outbound queues. If you are using the FORCE parameter, on the other hand, it is guaranteed that all selected queues will be restarted.

If a very high number of queues are paused in a system, or are stopped because of errors, we recommend that you activate the queues step-by-step. A large number of outbound queues with a large number of requests in them may have built up during the pause. If all of these queues are acti-vated at the same time, the system load can increase dramatically, and this may lead to a drop in performance.

You can check the status of selected or of all outbound queues using report program RSTRFCQ2.

Inbound Queues

There is a monitor available for the inbound queue as well as the outbound queue. You can access it using transaction **SMQ2**. Transaction **SMQ2** offers functions for inbound queues that are analogous to those of transaction **SMQ1** for outbound queues. To stop or restart the processing of inbound queues, you can use the report programs RSTRFCI1 (stop) and RSTRFCI3 (start). These report programs are the same, in terms of use and functions, as the report programs for outbound queues.

The status of selected or all inbound queues can be ascertained using report program RSTRFCI2.

The display of requests in the inbound queues is slightly different from that for outbound queues. Table 3.6 summarizes the information.

Column	Role
Clt	Client to which the queue is assigned
User	User under which the queue is being processed
Function module	Function module called in the system for processing
Queue name	Name of the queue in which the request is located
Date	Date on which the request was placed in the queue
Time	Time at which the request was placed in the queue
Status text	Error text, should an error occur in processing
TID	Transaction ID: An internal identifier is assigned to each request entering an inbound queue. The request can be traced in the system using this transaction ID.
Original TID	Original transaction ID: A transaction ID that the request that has entered the inbound queue held in the outbound queue of the sending system
Host	Name of the application server on which the request for the inbound queue was created
Tktn	Transaction that will be executed in the target system for processing
Program	Program that will process the request in the target system

Table 3.6 Meaning of the columns in the inbound queue display

In older APO releases and in APO 3.0 before support package 11, only outbound queues were used. Therefore, the inbound monitor cannot be used with these.

Table 3.7 below gives an overview of the most important states that a queue can assume.

Status	Meaning	
	Outbound queue	Inbound queue
Ready	Ready for processing. If the queue is stopped manually, the object also remains in this status.	Ready for processing. If the queue is stopped manually, the object also remains in this status.
Running	Processing	Processing
Stop	The queue was stopped manually with the help of transaction **SMQ1**.	The queue was stopped manually with the help of transaction **SMQ2**.
Waitstop	The object in this queue depends on objects in other queues, which must be processed before this one. One of these queues has been stopped manually.	The object in this queue depends on objects in other queues, which must be processed before this one. One of these queues has been stopped manually.
Waitupda	The processing sequence of this object contains a local update step. Before it can be sent, this step must be successfully completed. If an object is in this status for longer than a few seconds, this can lead to an update termination (check with transaction SM13).	–
Waiting	The object in this queue depends on objects in other queues, which must be processed before this one.	The object in this queue depends on objects in other queues, which must be processed before this one.
Executed	The object in the queue was processed, and is only awaiting confirmation from the target system.	–
Sysload	At the time of processing, there was no work process available in the source system for processing.	–

Table 3.7 Status of qRFC objects and what it means

Status	Meaning	
	Outbound queue	Inbound queue
Sysfail	A grave error occurred in the target system during processing, which led to termination. Double-click to view the error message. Other details on the error can be found in the target system (!) in the system log (transaction **SM21**) or in the list of runtime errors (transaction **ST22**).	A grave error occurred in the local system during processing. You can view the error message by double-clicking. Further details on the error can be found in the local system in the system log (transaction **SM21**) or in the list of runtime errors (transaction **ST22**).
Cpicerr	A network or communication error occurred during transfer to the target system. You can view the error message by double-clicking on the object. If necessary, you can also find further information in the local system log (transaction **SM21**) or in the developer trace (transaction **ST11**), in particular the gateway (dev_rd) and RFC connections (dev_rfc*).	Should a network problem or another temporary problem occur during the processing of a request in the inbound queue, the status **Cpicerr** is also set. In this way, in accordance with the settings for tRFC, the request can be processed again at a later point in time.

Table 3.7 Status of qRFC objects and what it means (continued)

If there are errors in processing a queue, the actual cause of the problem should always be resolved. Deleting a defective object from the queue only leads to inconsistencies in the dataset, and does not fix the actual problem. Deletions from queues are recorded in the system log of the corresponding application server of the system.

Trace and Log

For analytical purposes, transactions **SMQ1** and **SMQ2** offer the possibility of activating a *trace* and a *log* for processing individual or generic queues. All processing steps of a request are recorded in a trace. In the log, on the other hand, only errors are recorded. Both analysis methods should be used only in exceptional cases and, where possible, should not be used in production systems. Activating the log or the trace affects performance because it increases the write load.

To activate the trace or log, proceed as follows:

1. Start transaction **SMQ1** or **SMQ2**.
2. Select the queue of a client to be displayed.
3. From the menu, select **QRFC · Trace / Log · Activate**.

Then start the processing of the procedure to be logged. Once the procedure is complete, **deactivate** the recording immediately. The resulting log can be viewed using the function **Display**.

List 3.1 below shows a possible qRFC trace.

```
14.12.2001 Evaluation of qRFC trace                        1
-----------------------------------------------------------

===========================================================
QTYPE: OUTBOUND/S    DATE: 14.12.2001  TIME: 15:52:31
CLIENT: 800          USER: WILL
QDATE: 13.12.2001   QTIME: 08:42:59
TID: 0A108911030C3C185C0360F6               ORGTID:
QSTATE: SENDING    BJOB: N   QEVENT: N   DEST: T90CLNT090
EMESS : 00000001 / CFIP3168      / CIF_ORDER_INBOUND_30A
===========================================================
QTYPE: OUTBOUND/S         EXETIME: 00:00:01
DATE: 14.12.2001   TIME: 15:52:32
CLIENT: 800          USER: WILL
QDATE: 13.12.2001   QTIME: 08:42:59
TID: 0A108911030C3C185C0360F6               ORGTID:
QSTATE: SYSFAIL    BJOB: N   QEVENT: N   DEST: T90CLNT090
EMESS : Planned order 29513 is not designated for transfer
00000001 / CFIP3168          / CIF_ORDER_INBOUND_30A
===========================================================
```

Listing 3.1 Extract of a qRFC trace

The qRFC trace is created in a sending system, from an outbound queue. A block is written for each processing step. The receiving system works without inbound queues. The first step in processing the request was to send the request to the target system (QSTATE: SENDING). In the target system, function module /SAPAPO/CIF_ORDER_INBOUND_30A was called (see the last line in the first block). The header record /SAPAPO was basically omitted when recording. The name of the function module /SAPAPO... indicates that the target system was an APO system. When processing the request in the APO system using the function module, an error occurred in the target system. The status of the outbound queue in the source system changed to **Sysfail** (QSTATR: SYSFAIL). The error text that appeared was also transferred. With the help of the qRFC trace and the log, a queue's processing steps can be recreated in detail.

Recordings can be removed after the completion of the evaluation, using the **Delete** function from the **Trace** or **Log** menu. If the log created is very long, you should certainly ensure that it is deleted after the end of the analysis.

Event Triggering

Another interesting function of the qRFC is the ability to connect any function module, which can be automatically activated by pre-defined events. This function is also available for both inbound and outbound queues. From the menu of transaction **SMQ2** or **SMQ1,** select the function **Goto · QRFC administration** or use transaction **SMQE** to go directly to qRFC administration. In the following screen you can use **Event registration** to register selected queues (inbound or outbound) and connect any function module. To date, the following events are available:

▶ 1   After every successful LUW processing

▶ 2   LUW processing terminated and no batch job scheduled

▶ 3   LUW processing terminated (with or without batch job)

▶ 4   Option 1 and 2

▶ 5   Option 1 and 3

▶ A   On request (depending on program) and option 1

▶ B   On request (depending on program) and option 2

▶ C   On request (depending on program) and option 3

▶ D   On request (depending on program) and option 4

▶ E   On request (depending on program) and option 5

For example, if the processing of a queue is terminated, it is possible to execute a function module which sends a message with the error text to the system administrator. Event 2 can be used for this. The background job mentioned with the events refers to background jobs of the type ARFC: SYSLOAD1<Client><User>, which in the event of overload situations in the source system (termination with the message **Sysload**), is automatically scheduled to repeat the request. If the overload problems are temporary and can be handled with a renewed attempt at processing, you will not really need to be informed. For this reason, in our example, event 2 would be suitable. You would be informed only if the background job is not scheduled and this is therefore not a matter of a temporary overload problem. Details on the configuration of the background job to automatically repeat should load problems arise can be found in Section 3.5.1 of this Chapter and in SAPNet Note 437718.

3.6.4 R/3 System: Data Channel Monitor

Whereas the qRFC monitor reflects a somewhat technical view of the queues, within the dedicated R/3 systems, it is also possible to see an application view of the active data channels. For this, use transaction **CFP2** in the connected R/3 system. In the initial screen you can limit the view to the desired logical target system. Figure 3.8 shows the overview of the data transfer channels to an APO system.

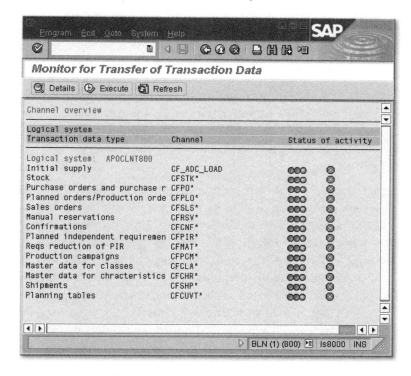

Figure 3.8 Data channels from an R/3 system to an APO system

A red light indicates when problems occur in a data transfer channel. By double-clicking on a selected channel, details on the data in this channel are displayed. As already presented in Table 3.2, certain business objects are assigned to each channel. Therefore, this overview is very useful for finding out which type of business objects cause problems. If the problems in the queue are not of a technical nature, you can use this monitor to determine the application module concerned.

Technical problems can certainly be repaired by the system administrator. Unfortunately, the problems may also be related to the application. An example of a frequent problem is customizing changes that are not allowed for in one of the systems involved. For example, if a new plant is created in an R/3 system, but this information has not been transferred to the APO system, an error occurs as soon as the first business object connected to this plant is transferred.

You should make certian that changes to customizing data can be carried out only in a manner that will make them consistent with all systems participating in the business system group.

3.6.5 Application Log

Both in the dedicated R/3 systems and in the APO system, an *application log xe "application log"* is written for transfer. As the name suggests, an application log supports the application view of the request. This tool is a starting point for analyzing problems in the application, particularly in the event of errors.

Customizing The degree of detail in the data transfer log can be configured in each sending system to suit each user. To do so, in the R/3 system, call transaction **CFGD** or **Logistics · Central function · Supply chain planning interface · Core interface Advanced Planner and Optimizer · Settings · User settings**, and in the APO system, call transaction **/SAPAPO/C41** or **Tools · APO Administration · Integration · Settings · User parameter**. The level of detail recorded in the application log can be configured individually for each user or generically for user groups. For the actual logging, you can choose between **No logging**, **Standard**, and **Detailed**, and you can also choose the number and content of the data records. To reproduce erroneous procedures, debugging can be activated for all processing steps or only for qRFCs. Application-specific recording details can also be defined. In the R/3 system, logging can be limited to qRFC requests. In production systems, logging should be switched off for all users. In this way, a note will be written to the application log only in the event of error. To deactivate application logging, enter a line with the value * in the **User** column so that the entry applies to all of the system's users. All other options in this line should be switched off. If you later need to temporarily activate logging for a selected user, you can overwrite the general setting with a special entry for this user.

When application logging is switched on, the requests are logged according to configuration. These entries can be viewed in the R/3 system via transaction **CFG1** or **Logistics · Central function · Supply chain planning interface · Core interface Advanced Planner and Optimizer · Monitoring · Application log**, and in the APO system via transaction **/SAPAPO/C3** or **Tools · APO Administration · Integration · Monitor · Application log**. You can use the transaction ID, as it is displayed in the queue monitors, to limit the display to selected procedures. Should you notice a problem in the queues, you can also use the transaction ID displayed there to get further application-specific details on the problem in the application log. In newer qRFC releases you can also branch directly to the application log by double-clicking on the error text in the qRFC monitor.

Display

The application log is written continuously. Deleting obsolete logs must usually be activated manually by the system administrator. Before doing so, the administrator must first confer with the relevant departments. The obsolete recordings should be deleted only after the departments concerned have checked the application log for possible errors. It is also possible to schedule the deletion of entries in the application log as a task of the department concerned. The application log can be deleted using the corresponding menu function **Delete entries**. It is easier, however to schedule a background job on the based on the report program SBAL_ DELETE, which is available in both R/3 and APO systems. The delete process can be configured as required. Normally, you should delete daily all entries that are more than 24 hours old. Deleting can also be done user-specifically, object-specifically, or depending on the transaction ID, for example. If the application log is not deleted regularly, in extreme cases this can lead to general performance problems in the system.

Delete

3.6.6 Alert Monitor RZ20 for qRFC

The monitors described to date (except for the qRFC alert monitors /SAPAPO/RCIFQUEUECHECK and /SAPAPO/RCIFINQUEUECHECK, which are available in APO systems), are operated manually, which means that error detection and notifying the appropriate persons do not occur automatically. Instead, the system administrator has to run the tools regularly and check for errors. The alert monitor integrated into SAP software (transaction **RZ20**) represents an easier way to check qRFC transfers. The connection of the qRFC was delivered with Basis support packages for:

▶ Basis release 4.5B with support package 47

▶ Basis release 4.6B with support package 35

▶ Basis release 4.6C with support package 26

▶ Basis release 4.6D with support package 15

▶ Basis release 6.10 with support package 08

The functions of the alert monitor mean that if threshold values are exceeded or if a defined problem case occurs, an alarm is triggered. As you know from alert monitors in general, for defined events, a message can also be sent to selected user groups, for example. The alert monitor also supports central monitoring. Any remote systems can be monitored by an alert monitor.

Scenario The following scenario could be implemented: Within the system group of R/3 systems, APO systems, and possibly also CRM systems, one system is defined as the central monitoring system. A test or quality control system would also suffice. This system should be available constantly. If the selected system is not a production system, it has the added advantage that production is not overloaded because of the additional load caused by monitoring. In this central system you should configure the alert monitor so that all information from the system group is collected there, as well as qRFC messages. By doing this, you gain a global view of the problems of the entire system group, and especially the activities for exchanging data. In the event of error, the alert monitor sends messages autonomously in accordance with configuration. The following information on qRFC requests is currently delivered to the alert monitor and can be evaluated:

▶ The number of qRFC requests in the outbound queues

▶ The number of qRFC requests in the inbound queues

▶ Error messages in the outbound and inbound queues

If pre-defined threshold values are exceeded, the alert monitor can send the corresponding warnings. In alert monitor customizing, you can configure separate subtrees for relevant clients. You can even select certain queues and create separate subtrees for them. This can be useful if one system sends to several other systems and, for example, you wish to control queues for CRM systems and APO systems separately. In addition, you can assign function modules to the defined subtrees, which are either executed every time the alert monitor gathers data, or only in analyzed cases of error. This can be useful if certain error situations do not need to be taken into account in queues, such as if the status **Stop** occurs in a queue. This status shows that a queue has been paused manually. Because this should normally be done only by the system administrator, there is no need to trigger an alert and, in some cases, send a message to yourself! You should therefore rate this status as uncritical and stop alerts.

Details on connecting the qRFC to the alert monitor can be found in SAP-Net Note 441269.

Concerning monitoring data transfer between R/3 and APO systems, a typical operating sequence can look like this:

Summary

1. The alert monitor **RZ20** is used as the central qRFC monitoring tool. Alternatively, the report programs /SAPAPO/RCIFQUEUECHECK and /SAPAPO/RCIFINQUEUECHECK, with clearly limited functions, can be used as quasi-alert monitors in the APO system.

2. If an error message appears in a queue or a certain number of requests in a queue is exceeded (possible only with **RZ20**), the alert monitor sets off an alarm and sends a message to the system administrator or the group of people responsible.

3. You should first check to see if the problem is technical with the queue monitors **SMQ1** or **SMQ2**. The technical problem is removed and the queue is started again, where appropriate.

4. If, on the other hand, the queue monitor shows that an application-related problem has occurred, the data transfer channel monitor (transaction **CFP2**) in the R/3 system is used to inform the corresponding department and to ask for help. In addition, transaction ID is used to look for related entries in the application log (transaction **/SAPAPO/C3** in the APO system or **CFG1** in the R/3 system).

5. Tools such as the system log (transaction **SM21**), the list of runtime errors (transaction **ST22**), developer traces (transaction **ST11**), or the gateway monitor (transaction **SM58**) can be used for further analysis.

6. If after all this, the cause of the error has still not been identified, the level of detail in the application log (transaction **CFGD** in the R/3 system or **/SAPAPO/C41** in the APO system) can be raised to debugging. The trace or log for qRFC (transaction **SMQ1** or **SMQ2**) can also be used.

3.6.7 Responsibility

When working with interfaces, as is undeniably the case with CIF, when planning and executing a project the question of who will be responsible for monitoring the interface always arises. With the integration of an APO system into a system landscape, the level of data transfer between the systems is multiplied. Data exchange is often an important prerequisite of the functional efficiency of the entire system group. Particular attention should therefore be paid to the functional efficiency of the CIF interface. It is especially important to define responsibilities clearly. In the event of problems with CIF, we can differentiate between technical problems and application-specific problems. As a result, solving problems is not only a concern of the systems administration group. A solution to the problem should be sought in collaboration with departments and technicians. In this situation, appointing people to be responsible for the interface has proven to be good practice. It is the responsibility of these people to build up the necessary information related to the business objects to be exchanged. They work on the interfaces between Basis and the applications.

4 liveCache Architecture

The liveCache is of particular importance to the APO system. In this chapter we will present its architecture and functions in greater detail. The theory forms the basis for understanding the practical administrative tasks that are associated with the use of the liveCache.

4.1 Basic Principles

The liveCache is a specific example of a *Database Management System* (DBMS). Part of the underlying technology is based on the database system SAP DB or ADABAS D, marketed by Software AG. As a result, readers familiar with ADABAS D or SAP DB will recognize some of the technology and administration tools, albeit in a slightly different form.

Nevertheless, SAP DB and the liveCache are only superficially comparable. SAP DB is a *relational database management system* (RDBMS). Data is stored on the hard disk. Performance is increased because parts of the data are kept in main memory areas. The data is held in tables, which are processed with SQL.

In contrast, with the liveCache, the main memory areas are of even greater importance. The hard disk areas only serve to increase security. All data is held in cache areas. Access to the liveCache and data processing normally requires no hard disk access. The difference is even clearer if we take into account the data retention and access methods. The liveCache supports object-oriented data management. While the liveCache does offer an SQL interface and relational data structures, access to data with SQL is reduced to a minimum. The SQL interface can still be used for communication with the SAP SQL standard interface, however. If required, the SQL interface can also be used by COM routines (LCApps).

In brief, the liveCache, like an RDBMS, is made up of memory areas (caches), hard disk areas, and processes. Figure 4.1 reflects this structure.

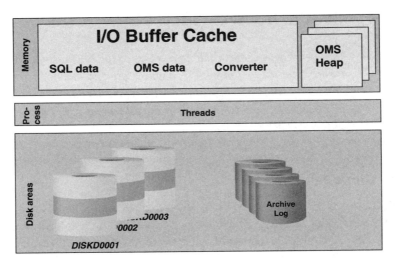

Figure 4.1 The basic architecture of the liveCache

4.2 Main Memory Management

First we will look at the main memory areas used permanently by the live-Cache. One of the largest main memory areas is the *I/O buffer cache*. It contains both SQL data and what is referred to as OMS (*Object Management System*) data. OMS data is treated like objects. The I/O buffer cache in turn contains other caches, which are used for management and process control, in the broadest sense. The cache area for SQL and OMS data is also known as a *data cache*.

4.2.1 SQL Data

Within the I/O buffer cache, access to SQL data from ABAP programs via the SQL interface is supported. As is common in RDBMS, this SQL data is arranged in tables, and, if necessary, in indexes. The SQL data and the area occupied by it in the I/O buffer cache are, however, of less importance. Only around 2–3% of the entire I/O buffer cache is usually used for SQL data, but this can vary greatly from one application to another.

4.2.2 OMS Data

The most important of the liveCache's innovations is the use of object-oriented methods. Access to object data, in the form of persistent C++ objects, is done from C++ application programs known as *LCApps* or *COM routines*. In contrast to the SQL data, which is organized in tables, object data is managed in containers, assigned as object memories to exactly one persistent C++ class of the object type. The data is processed not with the SQL interface from an ABAP program, but with the OMS interface. The advantage of this technology lies in the integration of application logic, in the form of LCApps, into the liveCache kernel. As a result, the somewhat costly communication and data transfer does not apply—which results in improved performance. In contrast to the data cache of an RDBMS, which always contains only the currently needed data, with the liveCache the I/O buffer cache is so large that, insofar as is possible, there is space for all of the OMS data. Metaphorically speaking, the liveCache is fully operated in the memory. This brings even greater performance gains.

The OMS data is kept in the I/O buffer cache; there is no physical separation of OMS and SQL data. The I/O buffer cache is managed in *pages* (blocks) of 8 Kb each. Each page is marked as to whether it contains SQL data or OMS data. From a technical point of view, the different pages for SQL and OMS data exist side by side. Figure 4.2 shows the logical structure of the liveCache. **Page**

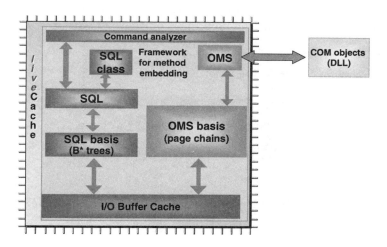

Figure 4.2 Structure of the liveCache

4.2.3 Converter

The *Converter* (see Figure 4.1) manages the pages. Allocation between physical page numbers in the hard disk areas and logical page numbers takes place in the converter. Applications can access only data with logical page numbers. During operation of the liveCache, the entire table of allocation between logical and physical pages is kept in the converter—in other words, in the memory.

The converter is also organized in pages. The size of the converter depends directly on the defined size of the hard disk areas of the liveCache. 1,861 entries for allocation between logical and physical pages can be stored in one page of the converter. At the same time, an image of this assignment is maintained on the hard disk areas of the liveCache in the form of a three-phase tree. This tree is needed for refilling the I/O buffer when the liveCache is restarted. For this reason, the root of the tree is maintained in a specially identified page in the hard disk areas which is known as the *restart record* of the liveCache.

4.2.4 Structuring of OMS Data

As described above, the I/O buffer cache is structured in pages. One page contains either SQL data or data on objects (OMS data). It can contain several objects of the same class. The data blocks are linked to each other with pointers. Multiple pages that go together, i.e., pages which contain objects of the same class, are grouped together in *page chains*. A *container* is assigned to each page chain (see Figure 4.3). Thanks to this partitioning, parallel access to page chains and, in turn, to objects of a class, is made easier.

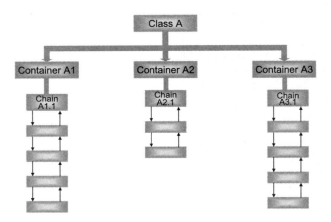

Figure 4.3 Page chains, containers, and classes

Persistent objects are formed by a COM routine as an object instance of a persistence-compatible class, and they exist beyond the runtime of the COM routine. A persistent object within a page is made up of a 24-byte *header* and the *data body*. The header contains all of the information necessary for converting the transaction logic, such as, "object is locked exclusively". The data body contains the actual application data. An object cannot be larger than one page, and is therefore limited to a maximum of 8 Kb. A page generally contains several objects of the same class. An exception to this is objects of variable length, which can have a maximum size of up to 2 Gb. Processing this type of object is much more "costly", however.

In general, the COM routines directly access the data body of an object with an *object identifier (OID)*. The liveCache manages the physical linking of pages. The application-related linking of objects is done by the application—that is to say, by the COM routines, which "know" where the necessary objects are located and which contain the necessary access logic. The OID is made up of a logical page number, the *position index (slot)* of the object within the page, and a version indicator (see Figure 4.3), which is necessary to be able to use an OID again.

Object identifier

Objects with unique keys represent a special type of objects. This key is used to look for the objects that match pre-defined data. The key can be seen as a point of entry from the relational world to the object-oriented world. With access via the key of an object, the application obtains the object identifier and can therefore use this OID to address the object directly. Access via the OID is thus the standard method of access for persistent objects.

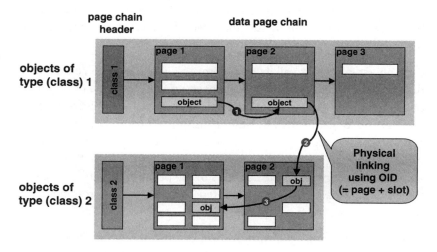

Figure 4.4 Using the object identifier

4.2.5 OMS Heap

The liveCache occupies another main memory during operation, in addition to the main memory areas described above. This is called the *OMS heap* (*private OMS cache*). In contrast to the I/O buffer cache, the OMS heap is allocated as required. To properly understand the background and the administration tasks described in the following chapters, it is essential that we take a closer look at the architecture and functioning of this technology.

Consistent view When a user starts a transaction, she would like to retain her data view until the end, independent of writing transactions. The liveCache supports these *consistent views* of data. Subsequent changes to data by another user do not change the data view of the first user. The same view is maintained until the end of her work. Technical conversion is carried out by copying the data required in each case at the beginning of the transaction in a cache exclusive to that user—the OMS heap of the liveCache.

Undo files Before making changes to an object, each writing transaction records the status of an object (*before image*) in what are known as *undo files*. Undo files are written to the I/O buffer cache, and can be used to rollback a transaction. (The term "file" here stands for page chains and should not be confused with operating system files.) One undo file is assigned to each open transaction. A record is kept of all undo files existing at one point in time, together with their transaction reference, in what are known as *history files*.

Each object is linked to all its before images, which may be contained in different undo files. With these references, you can trace the history of an object. The undo files exist until the before images of the objects stored in them are no longer needed by other consistent views and the write transaction has been successfully completed. If the write transaction is interrupted, the changes are rolled back with the help of the undo files. Should another transaction need the contents of the pages before the changes of the writing transaction are implemented, the transaction is re-directed to the before images in the undo files.

The OMS heap is managed with the help of hash tables. If an object needs to be accessed, it is first sought in the OMS heap, which is private to each user. If it is not found there, the OMS data body in the I/O buffer cache is searched. If it is not there either, it is copied from the hard disk areas in the OMS data body of the I/O buffer cache to the OMS heap. All changes to the object are then transferred to the OMS heap. The new status of the object is not transferred to the global I/O buffer cache yet. The OMS data from the OMS heap is not saved to the global I/O buffer cache until a transaction has been completed with a Commit.

Transactional Simulations

Transaction simulations (also called *named consistent view* or *version*) are a special case. A user can simulate all change activities on data, which means that the changes are implemented in the OMS heap, but are not yet definitively saved. Other users do not see these changes yet and their view of the data is maintained. Transactional simulations executed in the OMS heap are given an internal name.

Should the user decide to save the transactional simulation, and the starting data has been changed in the meantime by another user, the user can choose whether the operation will be broken off or a *merge* will be carried out. With a merge, the changes are rewritten, taking into account the changes that have been made to the starting data in the meantime. In this way, all the data is mixed. Normally the user selects a set of data relevant to planning—usually the data for which he or she is responsible. Then the planning steps are carried out; for example, the effects of an advertising campaign are tested. The user simulates certain actions. If the user is satisfied with the results, then he or she saves the planning steps. In practice, each user has his or her own delimited planning area. It is very unusual in an application to find two users drawing up plans for the same products, locations, and customers at the same time. As a result, there is very little danger that one user can permanently change the data of another user. Changes to the starting data of a transactional simulation are most likely brought about by transfers from the dedicated systems.

The size of the OMS heap depends on the currently processed data set. The "larger" a user's current transaction, the more data needs to be copied to the OMS heap, and as a result, the heap will grow. On conclusion of a transaction, the data in the heap is deleted and the area in the OMS heap is released. However, the memory area is not returned to the operating system. From the point of view of the operating system, the size of the OMS heap remains unchanged.

The size of the OMS heap

In defined circumstances, at what is known as the *savepoint*, the changed data, including the history files, is copied to the data areas on the hard disk (*data devspaces*) of the liveCache. At the savepoint the changes in the converter are also transferred to the data areas of the hard disk. As previously described, the converter is managed on the data devspaces as a three-

Savepoint

phase tree. If changes need to be made to this tree, at the time of the save-point the new tree is also saved in parallel. When the savepoint is success-fully completed, the old converter tree is replaced by the new one. The root nodes of the tree are converted into the restart record and the pages of the old tree are released. There is usually a ten-minute interval between two savepoints. The purpose of the savepoints is to secure the data in the hard disk areas of the liveCache.

Log queue All changes to data (SQL and object data) are recorded in the *log queues* in the I/O buffer cache. Log queues contain the after images of objects and SQL data. The size of the log queue is defined by the liveCache parameters `LOG_IO_QUEUE` in pages. Every time a page of a log queue is filled or a transaction sets a commit, the *archive log writer* is activated. The archive log writer reads the data from the log queue and transfers the changes to the archive log area (*archive log devspaces*) on the hard disk of the live-Cache.

Garbage collectors *Garbage collectors* release pages from the undo files—that is, they release all pages in the history files that are no longer needed to implement con-sistent views. The released pages are returned to free memory manage-ment on the I/O buffer cache. Garbage collectors activate every 30 sec-onds. The release procedure depends on the following criteria:

▶ The maximum level of the data cache is under 90%.
  The garbage collectors release the objects that are older than the old-est transactional simulation.

▶ The maximum level of the devspaces on the hard disk is under 90%.
  For security reasons, the data cache area of the liveCache is must be guaranteed to be secure in the devspace area at all times. If the devs-pace area becomes completely full, the liveCache is brought to a standstill. The garbage collectors intervene to prevent this by deleting all pages in the undo files that are not needed for a possible rollback of transactions. Pages that may be needed for consistent views are also deleted. This can lead to terminations of the type `too old OID` or `object history not found` if there is a user action. In this case, however, data security must be given highest priority. You should therefore avoid a maximum level of over 90% in the data areas of the liveCache.

Figure 4.5 summarizes the different memory areas. The I/O buffer cache is mainly made up of:

- OMS data
- History files
- Log queues
- SQL data
- Converter

The I/O buffer cache is a main memory area that is available to all users. The OMS heap is an additional, user-specific memory area.

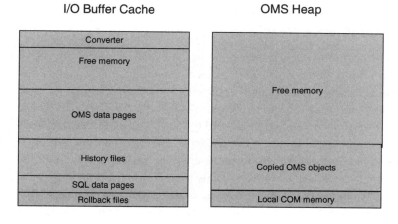

Parameter: CACHE_SIZE   Parameter: OMS_HEAP_LIMIT

Figure 4.5 Main memory area of the liveCache

The total size of the I/O buffer cache is defined by the liveCache parameter CACHE_SIZE. The size of the converter cache is automatically calculated from the configured size of the hard disk areas. In production operation, all history files should not amount to more than 30% of the size of the data cache.

The OMS heap is maintained as user-specific memory. It contains copies of objects from the I/O buffer cache and other local memories for processing data with COM routines. The OMS heap can grow; it reaches its maximum size when the memory required by the operating system for this purpose reaches the size defined with the liveCache parameter OMS_ HEAP_LIMIT. If the parameter is left at value 0, there is no logical limitation on the growth of the OMS heap. However, operating system parameters or limitations also have an effect when the main memory areas are being defined. With 32-bit Windows Enterprise Edition Advanced Server, the addressable limit is around 2.7 Gb. The I/O buffer cache of the live-Cache cannot exceed this limit. If there is an attempt to allocate more memory in the OMS heap, the COM routine is terminated (*Out of Memory Exception*). We have already looked at the possibilities of using PSE36 and AWE in Chapter 2. See SAPNet Notes 398665 and 384680 for further information on this topic.

For the purposes of improved scaling, the OMS heap can be divided into sub-heaps. The number of sub-heaps is defined by the liveCache parameter OMS_HEAP_COUNT.

4.3 liveCache Versions

There has been one decisive milestone in the evolution of the liveCache, which occurred with the change from liveCache release 7.2 to 7.4: when the liveCache and the associated applications were originally developed, it was assumed that the data volume managed by the liveCache in the main memory would remain small, and that only copies of the data to be processed would be held in the liveCache. The original data would be entirely saved in the APO DB. In the event of a crash and the loss of the liveCache, the liveCache could be reconstructed from the data in the APO DB. Quickly, however, it became clear that the data volume would be larger than originally assumed. The SCM system offered more possibilities than expected. The scope of the application grew, and with it the data volume to be managed. Re-creating data in the liveCache from the APO DB in the event of a crash could no longer satisfy performance requirements.

As a result, special logging was developed for liveCache 7.2 and parallel liveCache software was developed for release 7.4. (Because version 7.2 has not yet been fully replaced, we will indicate the differences between the two versions where appropriate. Unless otherwise stated, all of the following refers to release 7.4 of liveCache.) The I/O buffer cache area of live-Cache 7.2 is different from 7.4 in that it is physically divided into a *data cache* and a *converter cache*. Also, in liveCache 7.2, a consistent view is achieved by writing history files. If an object is changed, only its before image is written to a history file, and not the action, as in version 7.4. Rollback must be guaranteed until the completion of a modifying transaction; rollback files, which contain only pointers to the before images of changed objects, are written for this purpose. Rollback files and history files are actually pages in the data cache; history files are also user-dependent. In the event of a rollback, the data on the object is copied back from the history file. Before images must be maintained until the user has completed all operations on the objects in question. The objects can, of course, be changed several times by other transactions in the meantime. In this case, there may even be several versions of these objects in the history files. When a transaction is successfully completed, the history files that are then no longer needed are marked as obsolete; they are not released automatically. liveCache 7.2 also uses garbage collectors to release them.

The most significant difference between liveCache versions 7.2 and 7.4 lies in the fact that changes to OMS data are not recorded in the archive log areas; there is no physical logging for OMS data in liveCache version 7.2. An archive log is kept only for changes to relational data.

Normally, the history files should, again, not make up more than 30% of the data cache. The rollback files are so small that they can be ignored. The SQL cache takes up around 3%. The overall size of the I/O buffer cache is defined by the liveCache parameter DATACACHE.

In contrast to liveCache release 7.4, the garbage collectors are event-driven:

▶ The data cache is less than 90% full, but it lies above the value defined using the liveCache parameter _GC_DC_THRESHOLD.
The garbage collectors release the objects that are older than the oldest transactional simulation.

▶ The data cache is over 90% full.
All objects in the history files are checked to see if they are needed to ensure consistent views or if they can be released. Checking each object in the history file creates a higher load. As a result, the liveCache tries to avoid a fill level higher than 90%.

▶ The devspaces on the hard disk are under 90% full.
As with liveCache 7.4, the garbage collectors delete all pages in the history files that are not needed for any possible transaction rollback.

Garbage collectors are not active in liveCache 7.2 if the fill level is less than the _GC_DC_THRESHOLD parameter value. The standard setting for this parameter is 40, which indicates a fill level of 40%.

If the liveCache is very large, then you will also observe that the data cache will fill up steadily. If a level of 80% full is reached, the garbage collectors start to tidy up. The level will suddenly drop steeply and then start to grow again. This phenomenon is not critical to performance or problematic in other ways.

Checkpoint In release 7.2 of the liveCache, the data from the memory areas of the live-Cache is saved to the hard disk areas only at a certain time, which is represented by an event known as a *checkpoint*. The checkpoint must be manually triggered by the system administrator with the report program /SAPAPO/OM_CHECKPOINT_WRITE. A checkpoint establishes consistency between data cache areas and hard disk areas. For this, the data cache of the liveCache itself must be in a consistent state, that is to say, to execute the checkpoint no write transactions should be active.

We can distinguish between several different phases of executing a checkpoint. The first is *checkpoint wanted*. Because the checkpoint can be written only if all write transactions are complete, once a checkpoint is requested, no new write transactions are permitted. New write transactions are given wait status. As a rule, this method of procedure does not cause any problems, because the transactions are very short. It takes only a few milliseconds to set a checkpoint. The actual writing of the checkpoint depends on the changed data volume and can last up to a few minutes. While the checkpoint writes data, write transactions can begin work again.

Setting checkpoints can be problematic if a long-running write transaction is active when a checkpoint is requested. Figure 4.7 illustrates this situation. When the checkpoint is requested, some transactions are active (transactions 1, 3 and 4). The checkpoint cannot actually be written until transaction 3 has been completed. Transactions 5, 6, and 7 are not permitted during this time; they have to wait.

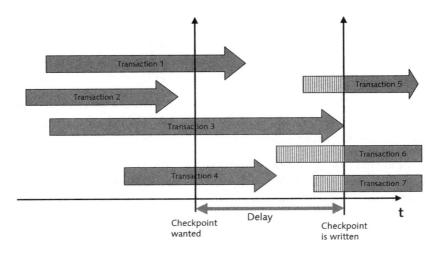

Figure 4.6 Writing a checkpoint

In the worst case, this can lead to an alleged system downtime because all users are waiting for the end of this single write transaction. Despite this, checkpoints should by no means be given up. Further details on configuration and problems related to checkpoints will be given in subsequent chapters.

4.4 Hard Disk Areas

The hard disk areas of the liveCache are less important to the actual processing of data than the familiar RDBMS. The data in the liveCache is saved to the hard disk areas only for reasons of security. To simplify things, we could say that the liveCache corresponds to a database operated on the main memory. Nevertheless, the hard disk areas of the liveCache must be administered, configured, and, in particular, made secure. This is comparable to the usual activities of the RDBMS administrator.

Among the hard disk areas of the liveCache we can differentiate between the *data devspaces*, which are for saving data, and the (*archive*) *log devspaces*, in which changes to data are recorded. Both log devspaces and data devspaces can be made up of several individual hard disk areas. In live-Cache release 7.2 the converter is also managed on a separate hard disk area (devspace), which is generally referred to as the *system devspace*.

In liveCache release 7.2, the archive log area of the liveCache is used only for the temporary storage of SQL data, which is needed in the event of a rollback of open transactions. From the point of view of the SAP DB, the Archive Log is configured as a demo log. This means that all associated SQL data in a log area can be overwritten again when a transaction has been completed. The data needed for a transaction rollback is kept only as long as the transaction remains open. The demo log guarantees only transaction consistency.

From the operating system's point of view, the hard disk areas are files. In Unix systems, *raw devices* should be used; with file systems, a certain amount of administration work is needed on the part of the operating system, so raw devices have a certain, although sometimes arguable, advantage. There are naming conventions for the individual hard disk areas, to help simplify administration (see Table 4.1). When using raw devices, a link—which adheres to naming conventions—to the raw device is used. On the operating system level, one user acts as administrator for the live-Cache *<liveCache name>adm*. In Unix systems, the liveCache hard disk areas used must feature at least authorization 660 for this user.

Hard disk area	Path	Naming convention
Data devspaces	/sapdb/<liveCache name>/sapdata/	DISKD<number>
Log devspaces	/sapdb/<liveCache name>/saplog	DISKL<number>
Only in liveCache 7.2: System devspace	/sapdb/<liveCache name>/dbsys	SYS

Table 4.1 Naming conventions of hard disk areas

The paths should be adapted accordingly for Windows systems.

The size of the data devspaces are defined when the liveCache is defined. The data devspaces in the liveCache should be considerably larger than the data cache area. How much bigger the data devspaces should be than the cache depends, first, on the change activity in the data cache, and, second, on the duration of transactional simulations. These key values determine the volume of the history files, which will have to be stored on the data devspaces if necessary. In extreme cases the data devspaces can be up to four times (eight times in version 7.2) the size of the data cache used by the liveCache.

In addition to the data and log areas, the liveCache needs further hard disk areas for organizational data and the actual liveCache software. Figure 4.8 shows the general directory structure in which the software, logs, configuration files, data, etc. of the liveCache are organized. You will find important logs for operating the liveCache in what is known as the *run directory* of the liveCache. These are particularly useful for analyzing errors (see Chapter 5). All program resources and the executable programs belonging to the liveCache are stored in the subdirectories *sapdb/programs*.

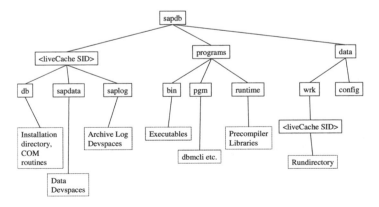

Figure 4.7 Directory structure of the liveCache

4.5 Processing Sequence

Figure 4.8 reflects the processing sequence for requests to the liveCache. As you know from the R/3 system, user requests are processed by work processes. In an APO system, however, the work processes not only work with the corresponding processes in the RDBMS of the APO DB, but also make requests to the liveCache. Each work process can log onto the live-Cache twice.

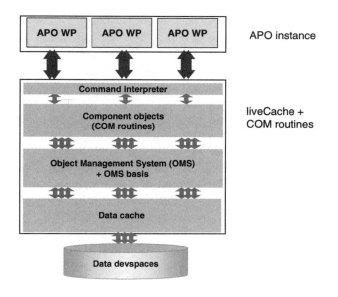

Figure 4.8 Operating sequences in the APO system

Requests to the liveCache are usually made with COM routines . The command interpreter undertakes the first analysis of the COM routine requests. When COM routines are called, the C++ programs, linked to the liveCache as *dynamic link libraries* (DLL), are started. In an ABAP program, calling a COM routine looks like this:

```
exec sql.
    execute procedure   "SAPTS_TRANS_SIM_CONTROL" (
       in   :ls_gen_com_params,
       out :lv_rc,
       in   :et_rc,
       in   :iv_simsession_method,
       in   :IV_TGRIDID,
```

```
   in  :IV_GET_CHANGED_VALUES,
   in  :ET_CHANGED_VALUE_TAB )
endexec.
```

The actual call to the COM routine is enclosed by `exec sql` and `endexec`. (This embedding is also used for calling native SQL commands.) COM calls are recognized by the subsequent `execute procedure`. Because this corresponds to the syntax for calling DB procedures (stored procedures), in statistics, calling COM routines is often equated with calling DB procedures. Each COM routine has a name, enclosed in inverted commas. For example, in the above example, the routine `SAP_TS_TRANS_SIM_CONTROL` is called. Input parameters are marked with the key word "`in`", and output parameters with "`out`". In contrast to SQL commands, no guidelines can be given for the duration of a COM routine. COM routines execute application logic, so runtime depends on the data volume to be processed and on the complexity of the application step.

COM routines use classes and methods, like those commonly used in C++. The objects used are stored in the I/O buffer cache or the OMS heap. The most important advancement over "conventional" C++ programs lies in the transaction logic adopted by the SAP DB database system, which includes dealing with locks.

4.6 Process Structure

As far as the operating system is concerned, the liveCache behaves like an individual process. This process is divided into several threads, which are called *User Kernel Threads* (UKT) in the liveCache. UKTs are in turn made up of tasks. The most important tasks are listed in Table 4.2.

Task	Role
Requestor	Manages process logon requests.
User<1-n>	The user tasks look after the requirements of the user processes logged onto the database. In the case of APO systems, these are work processes. If necessary, each APO work process can log onto the liveCache a maximum of twice, and is therefore assigned two user tasks.
Console	Observes the liveCache processes (kernel) and writes messages to log files. Provides information on liveCache procedures, such as I/O activities.

Table 4.2 UKTs and tasks of the liveCache

Task	Role
Data writer<1-n>	Writes the data from the cache areas to the hard disk areas in the event of a savepoint (liveCache 7.2: checkpoint).
AsDev<0-n>	Temporarily activated by the execution of backups. The number depends on the number of the data devspaces. AsDev0 coordinates the other AsDev<n>s.
Dev<0-n>	These dev-threads are needed depending on the devspaces on the hard disk. They execute the I/O operations on the hard disk areas. Dev0 coordinates the Dev<n> threads.
ALogWriter and OLogWriter	Writes the log information to the archive log area.
Server<1-n>	Executes the I/O operations during a backup of the liveCache.
Utility	Thread for executing administrative liveCache operations such as carrying out a backup.
GarbageCollector <1-n>	Keeps an eye on the COM cache and removes any obsolete object data.
Timer	Monitors time as part of lock management.

Table 4.2 UKTs and tasks of the liveCache (continued)

The number and type of tasks are set in configuration or by default. Several tasks can also be joined together in one thread by the liveCache. A thread can generally perform several tasks, but some tasks require a separate thread. A deciding factor for the number of threads is the number of CPUs available for the system, which is set by the parameter MAXCPU. If only the liveCache is run on the liveCache server, then MAXCPU can be equal to the maximum number of CPUs available; otherwise, MAXCPU must be reduced as appropriate.

4.6.1 Operation Modes

We can differentiate between three liveCache operation modes. In the *offline* mode, all processes or tasks of the liveCache are halted and the liveCache is not available; only changes to the liveCache parameters are possible. In the *admin* mode (version 7.2: *cold*), the liveCache is not generally available for the end user, but administrative tasks, such as backups, can be carried out. The operative mode of the liveCache is called *online* mode (version 7.2: *warm*).

4.6.2 Starting and Stopping

The liveCache is completely integrated into the APO system. For this reason, the liveCache should be started and stopped only under the direction of the APO system. If the liveCache is stopped using the tools described in the next chapter (DBMGUI or DBMCLI), the APO system receives information about this only on the next access, which fails. It is therefore recommended that you stop and start the liveCache using transaction **LC10: Monitoring • Administration • Operating**. To stop and start the liveCache from operating system level, the RFC-compatible function modules STOP_LIVECACHE_LVC and START_LIVECACHE_LVC can also be used. These function modules are also used by the report programs RSLVCSTOP and RSLVCSTART.

5 liveCache Administration Tools

In this chapter we will introduce you to the most important tools for the system administrator. For troubleshooting, the tools are usually used in combination, based on the problem. We demonstrate these tools' use by showing the solution to selected typical problems.

5.1 liveCache Monitor

The most important administration tools for the liveCache in the day-to-day use of your APO system are integrated into the APO system itself, which means that they are operated using the SAP GUI. You can access the special liveCache administration tools via **Tools · APO Administration · liveCache / COM Routines Tools · Monitor** or by calling transaction **LC10**.

Figure 5.1 shows the outline structure of the monitors combined in transaction **LC10**. You will find a more detailed overview of the functions grouped under transaction **LC10** in the appendix.

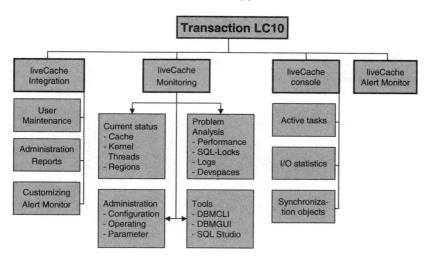

Figure 5.1 Overview of transaction LC10

In the initial screen of the monitor you will be asked for the liveCache's logical connection name. This tool can also be used as a central observation point for any other liveCaches of other APO systems. The liveCache connections allocated to the current APO system usually have the names

LCA and *LDA.* These names correspond to the two connections that each process forms with the liveCache.

In principle, an SAP system can manage and monitor any number of live-Caches. Even the name of transaction **LC10**, which does not include the addition **/sapapo/**, indicates that the transaction is also available in an R/3 system. In the case of an APO system, the connections for the liveCache are always *LCA* and *LDA.* These connections are already predefined; which of these connections is used for administration purposes is irrelevant. Use **Ctrl+F4** to open the connection's definition.

Should you wish to create a connection to another liveCache in your system landscape, equivalent entries for these liveCaches must be maintained. The procedure for doing this is as follows:

1. Enter a new logical name for the desired liveCache.
2. Press **Ctrl+F4**. A template appears, in which all necessary information is requested. Figure 5.2 shows this input template.

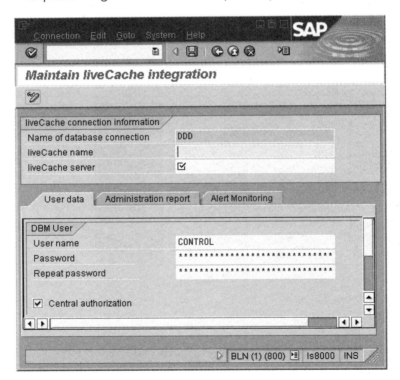

Figure 5.2 Customizing the connection to a liveCache

3. Enter the required information:

▶ The physical liveCache name is the name of the liveCache when the APO system is installed. The liveCache server name is also required.

▶ User data and possible administration reports must be maintained for each liveCache. User data means, on one hand, the administrator (database manager-user, DBM) and on the other, the "normal" liveCache user, under which the APO work processes also log onto the liveCache. Alert monitoring can also be activated if required. The alert monitor can be used only after the necessary settings have been customized.

▶ If the connection to be maintained is the connection to the liveCache assigned directly to the APO system, further actions can be scheduled for the initialization, starting, and stopping of the liveCache. Additional report programs can be executed before or after, such as sending a message or performing a consistency check. Enter the name of the report program, if you so require.

4. Save.

If the liveCache belonging to an APO system is initialized, the /SAPAPO/DELETE_ANCHORS report program must be executed after the initialization. When the liveCache is initialized, all transaction data, such as sales orders, is inevitably lost (see Chapter 4). In order to maintain consistency between the APO DB and the liveCache, the anchor tables in the liveCache (/SAPAPO/ORDKEY and /SAPAPO/ORDMAP) must be deleted. This is done by the report program /SAPAPO/DELETE_ANCHORS.

When you define a connection to a remote liveCache, please note that you may start and stop liveCaches of version 7.2 only from the corresponding APO system, because otherwise inconsistencies can occur. Report programs that you allocate to a connection will be executed in the local system and not in the appropriate APO system.

This function can be used in the older APO release 3.0 with liveCache 7.2. APO 3.0 is based on R/3 release 4.6C. With Basis support package 30 for 4.6C (APO 3.0), transaction **LC10** was revised and additional statistics and tools were added. Please take this into account if any menu paths given in this book differ from those in your system. The new structure and the extended performance of transaction **LC10** are already included in R/3 release 4.6D (APO 3.1).

You can take advantage of this circumstance in the administration of a live-Cache belonging to an older APO system 3.0, if an R/3 system 4.6D or 4.6C with Basis support package 3.0 is available in the system landscape. This R/3 system 4.6D or 4.6C can be used for the central monitoring of all liveCaches. In the R/3 release 4.6D in particular, connection of the live-Cache to the alert monitor **RZ20** is already included. You should also refer to SAPNet Note 415376.

The administration and monitoring scope of transaction **LC10** from Basis release 4.6D or from the Basis support package 3.0 for 4.6C covers the following areas:

▶ **Integration**

▶ **Monitoring**

▶ **Console**

▶ **Alert monitor**

Integration
All customizing settings that are concerned with the integration of the liveCache into the corresponding APO system are assigned to the **Integration** area. This is precisely the data mentioned above that has to be maintained when creating a new liveCache.

Monitoring
In the **Monitoring** area, you will find all the tools and monitors necessary for the routine operation of the liveCache. Monitoring is divided into the following subject areas:

▶ **Current status**

▶ **Problem analysis**

▶ **Administration**

▶ **Tools**

Entry to the general analysis is established via the display of **Properties**, into which you branch automatically when you call **Monitoring**. In addition to information on the version of the liveCache software used, the current status of the liveCache is indicated by a traffic light symbol. Green means that the liveCache is in *online* (*warm*) mode, and is therefore ready for use. Red, on the other hand, indicates the *offline* mode and yellow the *admin* (*cold*) mode.

A summary of statistics on the activities in the liveCache is presented in **Performance Overview** (see Figure 5.3).

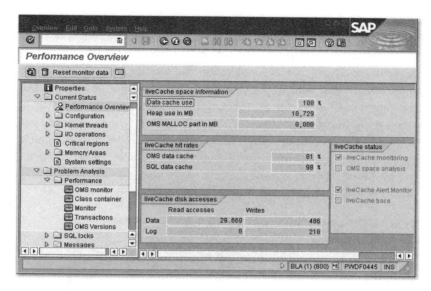

Figure 5.3 Overview of liveCache activities

When accessing the data cache, it is important to differentiate between the OMS data cache and the SQL data cache. The most important consideration in APO performance is the hit rate in the OMS data cache. It should not fall below 100%, and it should lie under 100% only for a short while after a restart. Write and read accesses to the liveCache have an effect on I/O activities. Over time you will learn to instinctively tell which values are normal for your liveCache operation. It would be impossible to give general guideline values.

In the area **Current Status**, you will also find all views on the liveCache threads, I/O activities, memory areas, hard disk areas, and so on. Performance statistics, logs, and messages are assigned to **Problem Analysis**. Administrative tasks include starting, stopping, and, if necessary, initializing the liveCache as well as configuration changes to devspaces and liveCache parameters. liveCache-specific tools can also be called fromm the APO system, if they are installed on the front-end PC. These are DBMGUI, DBMCLI, and SQL Studio, which will be discussed in greater detail below.

Monitors which allow a view of the runtime environment of the liveCache are available in the **Console** area. The term *console* has historical roots. In large computers and Unix systems the console was usually a selected screen or monitor that gave a specific view of the processes in the operating system. In the **Console** area—meant in this sense—you will find the monitors that reflect the activities of the liveCache from the point of view

Console

of the operating system. These include, for example, statistics on the activities of the UKTs, I/O activities, and the utilization of the memory areas for thread management (*regions*). The statistics in the **console** area are limited mainly to the display of measured values. Behind this is the DBMCLI tool, on the operating system level, which is called upon to provide information (see Figure 5.4). With the button **Enter commands**, commands can be immediately transferred to DBMCLI and executed. The commands that can be used are described in the SAP documentation on the liveCache or on SAP DB. Important commands are also listed in Table 5.4 and Table 5.5 later in this chapter. The same statistics, in an edited format, can also be viewed using **Current Status · Kernel threads** or **Memory Areas**.

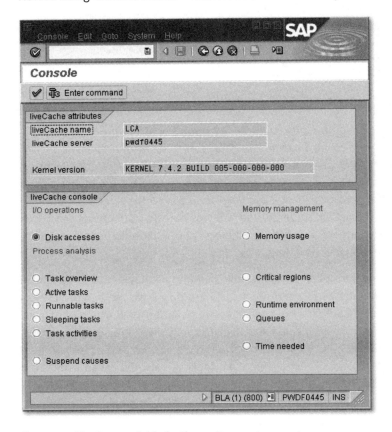

Figure 5.4 Monitors available for the runtime environment

Alert monitor   If the alert monitor from the **Integration** area of transaction **LC10** has been activated during customizing, you can branch directly to the live-Cache sub-tree in the alert monitor. For day-to-day operation and for detailed problem analysis of the liveCache, you should carry out regular monitoring using transaction **LC10 · liveCache: Monitoring**.

Messages and logs

By using the alert monitor and defining suitable threshold values for live-Cache operation, you will automatically be alerted to many problems. In the event of problems, the system messages and system error messages (**LC10 · Monitoring · Current Status · Problem Analysis · Messages · Core**) of the liveCache provide particularly useful information. A separate log is managed for the initialization of the liveCache, which you can view using the transaction **LC10 · Monitoring · Current Status · Problem Analysis · Logs · Operating · Current**. The displayed logs are read from files in the operating system, which means that even without using APO system resources, they can be viewed on the liveCache server, using the corresponding operating system commands. Table 5.1 shows the corresponding allocations.

Please take care that at each restart or attempted restart of the liveCache, the file *knldiag* is copied to the file *knldiag.old* and a new *knldiag* file is created. If the file *knldiag* contains important information, you should also create a backup copy of the file in good time. The initialization log *lcinit.log* is re-written on each initialization. The file *knldiag.err*, on the other hand, is run all the time. It contains all error messages that have occurred during the operation of the liveCache. As system administrator, you must take care that the file is not too big and you should delete it every now and then as necessary.

Contents	File	Path
Current messages	*knldiag*	*\sapdb\data\wrk\<liveCache-Name>*
Old messages	*knldiag.old*	*\sapdb\data\wrk\<liveCache-Name>*
System error messages	*knldiag.err*	*\sapdb\data\wrk\<liveCache-Name>*
Initialization log	*lcinit.log*	*\sapdb\<liveCache-Name>\db*

Table 5.1 Important liveCache logs

The area **Administration · Configuration** is divided into the configuration of the data area and the log area, and the parameters of the liveCache. Based on the architecture of the liveCache, *data area* refers to the number and size of the data devspaces in the liveCache. Figure 5.5 shows a live-Cache made up of five data devspaces.

Configuration

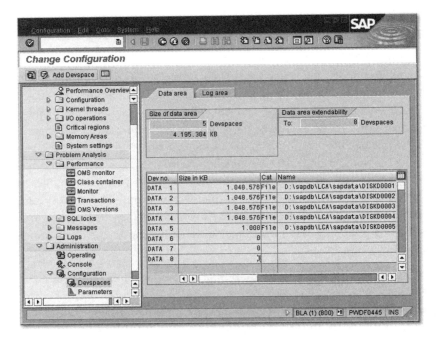

Figure 5.5 Configuration of the data area

The term *log area* here actually refers to the physical log areas on the hard disk. The log area and data area can be extended online from this monitor. The button **Add Devspace** is provided for this purpose. In this case, "enlarge" means that a new data devspace or log devspace will be added. The number of devspaces that can be added is limited by the parameters MAXARCHIVELOGS and MAXDATADEVSPACES. You can find an overview of all currently valid parameters of the liveCache under **Administration · Configuration · Parameter**. These parameters can be changed in any mode of the liveCache, but they do not come into effect until after a restart.

5.2 Database Manager

On the operating system level, the liveCache offers its own administration tool, the *database manager* (DBM). The DBM functions on the basis of a client/server architecture. What is referred to as the *DBM server* is run on the server on which the liveCache is operated. It is responsible for the actual retrieval of data. Two front-end interfaces are available to users: a graphical user interface, the DBMGUI, and a command-oriented variant of DBMCLI.

The SAP DB and any remote liveCaches can be managed using DBMCLI and DBMGUI. It is recommended that you make this software available on the system administrator's work station as well as on the liveCache server. DBMGUI is available only for Windows systems, unfortunately. The newest version of this software is available free on the *sapserv<x>* engines of SAP AG. You will find them at */general/sapdb/GUI_COMPO-NENTS/<release>/dbm<rel>.exe*. DBMGUI is upwardly compatible, which means that older versions of a liveCache or an SAP DB can be administered by a newer DBMGUI. Details on availability and the installation of the DBMGUI can be found under SAPNet Note 386714.

5.2.1 DBM Server

In order for front-ends, such as DBMGUI and DBMCLI, to be used for live-Cache administration, the communication server *vserver* must be activated for non-local communication with the liveCache on the liveCache server. To do so, you should proceed as follows:

1. Log onto the liveCache server as user *<liveCache ID>adm*.

2. Enter `x_server start`.

The *vserver* can be exited as required using

```
x_server stop
```

DBMGUI or DBMCLI commands are passed on to the DBM server using the communication server *vserver*. The DBM server communicates with the liveCache kernel, and looks after the execution of requests coming in from DBMCLI or DBMGUI. It is recommended that you keep the communication server permanently active.

5.2.2 DBMGUI

After executing these steps, DBMGUI can be called on any other server.

With the help of the DBMGUI (see Figure 5.6), any number of liveCache instances can be administered. The particular liveCache must be registered so that DBMGUI can work with the corresponding DBM server.

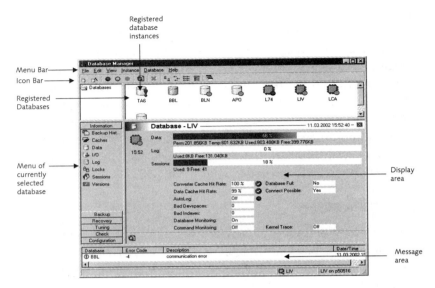

Registered
database
instances

Menu Bar
Icon Bar

Registered
Databases

Menu of
currently
selected
database

Display
area

Message
area

Figure 5.6 DBMGUI

To do so, you should proceed as follows:

1. From the menu, select the DBMGUI **File · Register Database**.
2. Enter the name of the liveCache server and confirm. A list of all live-Cache or SAP DB instances on this server will be displayed.
3. Select the liveCache instance to be managed.
4. Change to the **Register** function.
5. Select any meaningful name for the liveCache to be administered. It is usually recommended that you use the actual name of the liveCache, as set during installation.
6. Enter the name and password of the DBM user.
7. Click on OK. Registration is now complete. The liveCache instance is displayed in the area of the registered database instances.

The most important administration areas are:

▶ **Backup**

▶ **Recovery**

▶ **Monitoring**

▶ **Configuration**

If you are using liveCache 7.2, some functions of database administration, such as some backup functions, are of little or no significance. Only saving with a checkpoint is relevant for liveCache 7.2. You cannot do backups using DBMGUI or DBMCLI. Therefore, restore is relevant only when using APO resources in the event of a recovery. Also, you should start and stop liveCache 7.2 only from the APO system.

Below, we will describe the execution of a backup of liveCache devspaces and the subsequent recovery.

5.2.3   Defining Medium

The first step in carrying out a backup is to define a medium. By *medium* in the liveCache and the SAP DB environment, we refer to a description of, for example, a tape device and the tape used. It may also be the description of a file in the network that will be used as the target of the backup.

Table 5.2 shows the properties that must be set in the definition of a medium.

Property	Meaning
Name	A name for the medium. Can be chosen freely. This name can be used, for instance, to address the actual tape station and the tape located in it.
Location	Device driver or concrete name with a file path
Device type	Type of the medium: File, tape or pipe
Backup type	*Complete* – Complete backup of the liveCache *Incremental* – Only those pages changed since the last complete backup are saved *Log* – Backup of the archive log devspaces *AutoLog* – Medium for automatic backup of the log area
Overwrite	The contents are either overwritten or not.
Autoloader	When using a device with autoloader functions
OS command	Once the backup is complete, an operating system command can be executed. This command can trigger, for example, a change of tape in the autoloader station.

Table 5.2 Properties of a medium

When defining a medium, you set the type of backup for which the medium will later be used. Only complete backups are supported for live-Cache 7.2. From liveCache version 7.4 on, however, archive logs are also written and must be saved.

To define a medium, proceed as follows:

1. In the DBMGUI menu, select **Instance · Configuration · Backup Media**.
2. Call **Backup Media · New · Medium**.
3. Enter a unique, distinctive name for the new medium.
4. Record the properties for the medium, as described in Table 5.2. This is done in two steps:
   - ▶ Enter the characteristics in the first screen template.
   - ▶ Select **Extended** to move on to the second part. In this area you should enter, as appropriate, the size of the medium and whether any backups already on it should be overwritten.
5. Save the data. You have now defined a new medium. It will appear in the list of all defined media.

Medium: Pipe It is not absolutely necessary that the backup medium have a local tape device or file. For example, it is possible to write in a pipe, in order to connect another backup tool from an external manufacturer. The only prerequisite is that this tool be able to read from a pipe.

Backint External security tools such as Tivoli, Legato, and ADSM are often used when operating the software in a computer center. In this case, it is necessary to backup the liveCache using the external security tool. To secure Oracle databases with tools from an external manufacturer, for example, the *Backint* interface is used. A program called *backint* prepares the data to be backed up. For Oracle databases, the manufacturer supplies this type of program as *Backint for Oracle*. If this interface is already used in your system, you can also use it to backup the liveCache. To do this, you backup the liveCache in a pipe as follows:

1. Using the DBMGUI, define a specific medium, the name of which should begin with "BACK".
2. The medium type is pipe. In Windows systems, pipes are created with `\\.\PIPE\<name>`.
3. A special *backint* adapter program is supplied for the liveCache in the liveCache's */sapdb/<SID>/db/bin* directory. So that the program can be found when the backup is being made, you must create a configuration file which should contain the following entries, at least:
   - ▶ BACKINT
     The full path of the adapter program to be used for the liveCache (in Unix, for example, */sapdb/<SID>/db/bin/backint*)

- ▶ INPUT
  File through which you can communicate with *Backint for Oracle*
- ▶ OUTPUT
  File through which you can communicate with *Backint for Oracle*
- ▶ ERROROUTPUT
  File through which you can communicate with *Backint for Oracle*
- ▶ PARAMETER-FILE
  Configuration file of *Backint for Oracle*

4. Assign the path and the name of this configuration file to the environment variables `BSI_ENV`.

The *backint* adapter program transforms the data backup of the liveCache into the data format expected by *Backint for Oracle*.

For further details on this procedure, see SAPNet Notes 338681, 338903, and 387583. SAPNet Note 119863 contains a list of all supported external backup tools for the liveCache. Manufacturers of external backup tools also plan to produce a special *Backint for SAP DB* that can be used for the liveCache, making the *backint* adapter program unnecessary. However, it is anticipated that *Backint for SAP DB* will need to be be obtained from the manufacturer separately.

Several defined media can be grouped together in a *media group*. All media in a media group can then be saved in parallel during a backup, a method which leads to an approximately linear improvement in performance. That is to say, saving to two media at the same time is about twice as fast as saving on one medium at a time, and so on. **Media groups**

5.2.4 Backup

Defining media is a prerequisite for carrying out backups of data devspaces and log devspaces. The relationship between data saving and log saving is similar to other RDBMS. For liveCache 7.4, the backup types used in media definition are also supported:

▶ **Complete**
A complete backup of the data area in the liveCache is carried out.

▶ **Incremental**
Only those pages in the data area of the liveCache that have changed since the last complete backup are saved. In the event of a recovery, first the complete backup is re-saved and then the incremental backup is restored.

▶ **Log**
The data in the archive Log area is saved.

▶ **AutoLog**
By activating this mode, a backup of the archive log devspaces is automatically started as soon as the log is around 30% full. You can also use the liveCache parameter LOG_SEGMENT_SIZE to divide the archive log area into larger segments. However, a single segment cannot take up more than 50% of the entire archive log, or automatic backup of the archive log area would then always be started after one segment has been filled.

From the perspective of performance, it would be ideal if the log devspaces that make up the archive log were the same size. The size of the log segments should correspond to the size of the log devspaces, so that the number of log segments is the same as the number of log devspaces. Generally, the liveCache should be operated with the *autolog* option active, because this is the most secure method of preventing the log area from becoming too full.

For liveCache release 7.2, only the *complete* backup type is supported. There is no *autolog* option, because liveCache 7.2 does not work with this type of logging. In the event of a recovery, the last complete data backup has to be brought in first. After this, the incremental backups (optional) are restored, and finally the backups of the logs, in sequential order.

Carrying Out a Backup

A backup of liveCache 7.4 is carried out as follows:

1. Call **Instance · Backup · Complete**.
2. Select the desired backup type.
3. From the list of defined media, select the medium or media group appropriate to the selected backup type.
4. Click on the **Next Step** icon.
5. Check the data you have given once again. Start the backup by clicking on the **Start** icon.

The progress of the backup is continuously displayed in the DBMGUI. If the backup cannot be completed successfully, a message is displayed on the screen. **Instance · Backup · History** gives you an overview of all backups carried out and any errors that have occurred.

Backups can be carried out in either *cold* (*admin*) or *warm* (*online*) mode. The content of both types is the same. If the liveCache is first changed to *cold* (*admin*) mode, however, work with the liveCache is interrupted for the user. As a result, the entire APO system cannot be used. This is one reason why you should work out the backup strategy with the relevant departments. A backup in *warm* (*online*) mode should, when possible, be carried out at times of low load in liveCache operation. In any case, a backup always involves increased input, and output activities and performance may suffer as a result.

The procedure for the liveCache backup described above cannot be used for version 7.2, since it would lead to inconsistencies. Backup of liveCache 7.2 is described in Chapter 6.

5.2.5 Recovery

With liveCache recovery it is important to differentiate between releases 7.2 and 7.4. Release 7.4 functions like familiar RDBMS. You start by recovering the database backup and then follow with the log information. These actions are completely covered by the DBMGUI. With release 7.2, only the database backup can be recovered with the help of the DBMGUI. From there the recovery has to be continued from the APO system (see Chapter 7). To recover a liveCache backup, use the DBMGUI and proceed as follows:

1. Ensure that the underlying source of error, such as a defective hard disk, has been dealt with.
2. Start the DBMGUI for the liveCache.
3. Select the relevant liveCache by clicking on it.
4. Select the icon with a yellow signal. By doing so, you are changing the liveCache to *cold* mode.
5. Call **Instance · Recovery · Database**.
6. Select the option **Restore last backup**.
7. Ensure that the backup is available on the medium to be selected.
8. Select **RecoveryDatabase · Next Step**. You will be offered the last successfully completed backup.
9. Confirm the selected backup.
10. Select **RecoveryDatabase · Start**. The backup is then recovered.

    Up to this point, the recovery procedure is the same for liveCache versions 7.4 and 7.2. For liveCache version 7.2, the recovery now has to be continued from the APO system (see Chapter 7). You can proceed with the following step only if you are using version 7.4.

11. On successful completion of this procedure, the liveCache can be transferred to *warm* mode using **RecoveryDatabase · Restart**.

   With liveCache 7.4, the user is then required to provide the incremental backups or log backups needed to complete the recovery. If the current log data is still available in the log devspace, this is automatically recognized and the request for further backups does not apply.

5.2.6   Maintaining Parameters

A range of parameters is available for liveCache configuration. In normal operation, only a few of them are relevant in the liveCache environment, but because of particular circumstances, SAP Support may advise you to implement additional parameters. In general, the parameters are adapted using transaction **LC10 · liveCache: Monitoring · Administration · Configuration · Parameter**. You can find a history of all changes made to liveCache parameters using transaction **LC10 · liveCache: Monitoring · Current Status · Configuration · Parameter**.

Parameters can also be set using DBMGUI. To do this, select the desired liveCache and then select **Configuration · Parameters**. The most frequently used parameters are shown in the initial screen. To view further parameters you can select the icon **Show Extended and Support Parameters**. It is not recommended, however, that you change these parameters without consulting SAP Support. The most important parameters are listed in Table 5.3.

Parameter	Meaning
CACHE_SIZE (in 7.2 DATA_CACHE)	The size of the data cache available, in pages
INSTANCE_TYPE	Set at *LVC* for the liveCache
KERNELVERSION	Automatically determined by the system
LOG_MODE	Determines the log mode: *single* for a single writing of the log or *dual* for mirrored writing of the log
LOG_SEGMENT_SIZE	Size of the log segment in pages; if the value is 0, the entire log area is treated as one segment

Table 5.3 Important liveCache parameters

Parameter	Meaning
MAXARCHIVELOGS	The maximum number of log devspaces allowed
MAXBACKUPDEVS	The maximum allowed number of media in a media group on which backups can be made in parallel
MAXDATAPAGES	The maximum number of pages allowed in liveCache data devspaces
MAXCPU	Establishes how many of the total server CPUs can be used by the liveCache. This parameter is particularly important if several applications are operated on the liveCache server. See also SAPNet Note 425051.
MAXLOCKS	The maximum number of locks available
MAXUSERTASKS	The maximum number of connections allowed to the live-Cache. You should bear in mind that each work process logs on twice to the liveCache. For DBMGUI and so on, additional connection possibilities are needed.
RUNDIRECTORY	Working directory of the liveCache; contains logs such as *knldiag, knldiag.err*

Table 5.3 Important liveCache parameters (continued)

liveCache parameters can also be changed with DBMCLI commands. Please note that no changes to parameters come into effect until the live-Cache has been stopped and restarted.

5.3 DBMCLI

The command-oriented front-end DBMCLI is particularly suitable for use in shell scripts, for purposes such as requesting status. It can also be executed within ABAP programs as an external command. In principle, all requests and administrative tasks that can be executed in dialog mode with DBMGUI can also be done with DBMCLI.

The syntax for calling DBMCLI is as follows:

```
dbmcli -d <liveCache ID> -n <liveCache Server>
-u <liveCache user, password> <Command-Specifics)>
```

The options -d and -n are for logging onto the desired DBM server. Log onto the liveCache with -u. For administrative purposes, the user should use *control* (default password *control*). The actual tasks are transferred to the DBM server with the help of the command specifics. Table 5.4 shows the most important options of the DBMCLI commands.

Command type	Option	Command	Entry
List of all possible DBMCLI commands		`help`	
SQL statement	`-uSQL <sqluser, password>` e.g. `sapr3,sap`	`sql_execute`	`<SQL-Statement>`
Administration command	`-u <control user, password>`	`—`	`<Administrationskommandos>`
Set parameters		`param_directput`	`<Parametername> <Wert>`
Display parameter		`param_directget`	`<Parametername>`
Display all parameters with their values		`param_directgetall`	
Check parameters		`param_checkall`	
Display status	`-u <control user,password>`	`<Show-Kommando>`	

Table 5.4 DBMCLI options

With the help of options `-uSQL sapr3,sap sql_execute <SQL-Statement>` any SQL requests can be made to the liveCache. There are several *show commands* for requesting the status of the liveCache. You will find the most important of these listed in Table 5.5. In older versions of SAP DB, on operating system level, the program `x_cons <SID> <Show-command> [<Refresh Period in s>]` was also used locally on the database server. It is still available today in part and can still be used.

Command	Meaning
`Show version`	Displays the version of liveCache
`Show tasks`	Displays all liveCache tasks and their status on Windows NT
`Show active`	Displays all active liveCache tasks

Table 5.5 Additions for the console

These commands can also be used in transaction **LC10 · liveCache: Console**.

The most important administration commands, such as starting and stopping the liveCache and starting backups, are listed in Table 5.6.

Command	Meaning
`backup_start` `<backup_medium>` `RECOVERY DATA`	Executes a backup of the liveCache data devspaces. `<backup_medium>` indicates a backup medium that was previously best defined with DBMGUI.
`backup_save_state`	The status of the currently running backup.
`backup_history_ list` `<options>`	List of all executed backups. The list can be specialized and limited with the help of `<options>`. Possible options include: `-k <keyword>` Only rows that contain the specified keyword are shown. `-c <rows>` Only the named rows are listed.
`db_start`	Transfers the liveCache from *offline* mode to *cold* mode.
`db_restart`	Independent of the current mode, the liveCache is transferred to *offline* mode and then to *warm* (operational) mode.
`db_cold`	Independent of the current mode, the liveCache is transferred to *cold* mode.
`db_warm`	Independent of the current mode, the liveCache is transferred to *warm* mode.
`db_offline`	The liveCache is transferred from *warm* mode, through *cold*, and then to *offline*.
`autosave_stop`	Stops the **AutoLog** option.
`autosave_start`	Starts the **AutoLog** option.
`autosave_show`	Displays the status of the **Autosave Log** option.

Table 5.6 Administration commands

Starting, stopping, and saving liveCache 7.2 can be done only from the APO system. The use of DBMGUI or DBMCLI in these cases would lead to inconsistencies. Please see SAPNet Note 326073 on starting and stopping liveCache 7.2.

5.4 SQL Studio

As explained above, the liveCache supports an SQL interface. Much like SAP DB, the interface can be used with the tool *SQL Studio*, which is is available for all Windows systems. For purposes of analysis it should be available on the administrator's PC, at least. The software for SQL Studio is available on the SAP servers *sapserv<x>*. You can find them at */general/sapdb/GUI_COMPONENTS/<release>/sqlstd<rel>.exe*. You will also find details on SQL Studio installation and availability in SAPNet Note 386714.

Most of the data in the liveCache is object-oriented. Of course, this cannot be accessed with SQL.

The SQL interface is of particular interest for evaluating statistical data on liveCache usage. Examples of important statistics tables in the liveCache are presented in Appendix A.

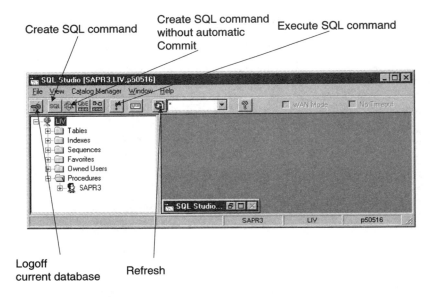

Figure 5.7 SQL Studio

Figure 5.7 shows the initial screen of SQL Studio. First you must select the desired liveCache. Select the icon with a key. In order to work with the SQL interface of the liveCache, you will need a user ID (see Figure 5.8).

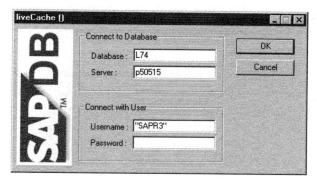

Figure 5.8 Logging onto SQL Studio

Normally, liveCache user *SAPR3* should be used.

5.5 Connecting to SAPNet

In problem situations, such as the recovery of the liveCache, you may need to allow SAP AG employees or partners to have direct access to the liveCache or the liveCache server. For such purposes, a special connection type should be set up in the SAPNet, under the name *SAP DB Connection*. To do this, log onto SAPNet. Create another connection, of the type SAP DB Connection, to your liveCache server. This connection allows remote access to the liveCache with the help of the DBMGUI. TCP/IP port 7269 is used for this; this port must be explicitly released in the *SAPROUTERS* configuration file named *SAPROUTTAB*. You will find details for the configuration of this connection in SAPNet Note 202344.

It is also advisable to add an SQL Studio connection to your liveCache.

5.6 Problem Analysis

In the following section, some typical examples of problems are presented to illustrate the use of the different tools and analysis tools. These examples should give you an idea of how the administrative tasks are resolved.

The liveCache Does Not Start

Symptom
The liveCache should have started, but has not.

Analysis
The liveCache's starting procedure is logged in the system messages in the file *knldiag*. This file is located in the directory */sapdb/wrk/<liveCache*

name>, or you can view it from the APO system using transaction **LC10** · **Current Status** · **Problem Analysis** · **Messages** · **Core**.

Background

All system messages are stored in the file *knldiag*. This includes not only messages regarding the starting procedure, but also messages from the current operation, such as writing the savepoint (also called the checkpoint in 7.2), or messages on the execution of backups. You should bear in mind that on every attempt to restart, the current *knldiag* file is copied to *knldiag.old* and a new *knldiag* file is created. Error messages are also continuously written to the *knldiag.err* file.

Solution

We cannot give you one general solution for unsuccessful restart. The messages in the file *knldiag* usually give only a reference to the problem.

```
12-28 15:24:38       0x5CC       19837 MEMORY
3370 Pages allocated for DATA CACHE at 0x0C7A0000
12-28 15:24:38       0x5CC       54003 dynDATA
DATA_CACHE_ PAGES       :    3370
12-28 15:24:38       0x5CC       54003 dynpool
B20_DATACACHE_ CB       : 229160
12-28 15:24:38       0x5CC       54003 dynpool
DATACACHE num cblocks   :    3370
12-28 15:24:38       0x5CC       54003 dynpool
DATACACHE cblock size   :      68

...
12-28 15:24:48       0x5CC       19837 MEMORY
3370 Pages allocated for DATA CACHE at 0x26DA0000
12-28 15:24:50       0x5CC       19837 MEMORY
3370 Pages allocated for DATA CACHE at 0x28800000
12-28 15:24:51       0x5CC       19837 MEMORY
3370 Pages allocated for DATA CACHE at 0x00000000
12-28 15:24:51       0x5CC ERR 18880 MEMORY
Could not allocate memory 27607056 bytes, rc = 1455,
( vos57.c:207 )
12-28 15:24:51       0x5CC       54003 dynpool
DYNP_B20_DATACACHE      :7479284
12-28 15:24:51       0x5CC       54003 dynDATA
DYND_B20_DATACACHE      :  60926
12-28 15:24:51       0x5CC       19616 DEVIO
Detaching devspace 'C:\sapdb\LIV\dbsys\SYS'
```

```
12-28 15:24:51        0x590      19614 DBSTATE
I/O thread for 'C:\sapdb\LIV\dbsys\SYS' stopped
12-28 15:24:51        0x5B0      19618 DEVIO
Single I/O detach, 'C:\sapdb\LIV\dbsys\SYS', UKT:3
12-28 15:24:52        0x5CC      19616 DEVIO
Detaching devspace 'C:\sapdb\LIV\sapdata\DISKD0001'
...
12-28 15:24:52        0x2AC      19614 DBSTATE
I/O thread for 'C:\sapdb\LIV\sapdata\DISKD0003' stopped
12-28 15:24:52        0x5CC      19616 DEVIO
Detaching devspace 'C:\sapdb\LIV\sapdata\DISKD0004'
12-28 15:24:52        0x5C       19614 DBSTATE
I/O thread for 'C:\sapdb\LIV\sapdata\DISKD0004' stopped
12-28 15:24:52        0x5CC      19616 DEVIO
Detaching devspace 'C:\sapdb\LIV\saplog\DISKL001'
12-28 15:24:52        0x754      19614 DBSTATE
I/O thread for 'C:\sapdb\LIV\saplog\DISKL001' stopped
12-28 15:24:52        0x5CC      19651 CONNECT
Connection released, T5
```
Listing 5.1 Extract from a kernel log (knldiag)

List 5.1 shows an extract from a kernel log in which the liveCache was unable to start. According to the parameter CACHE_SIZE, an attempt was made to allocate memory. However, insufficient memory was available on the server (Could not allocate memory...). As a result, the starting process failed. The devspaces and threads were stopped again.

Shortage of Space in Cache Areas

Symptom
A shortage of space in the cache areas of the liveCache always leads to a noticeable loss of performance. Capacity utilization should therefore be checked regularly. This is always necessary after extending the data range of the APO system.

Analysis
The liveCache's cache should be large enough that read accesses to the hard disk areas rarely occur. To check this, proceed as follows:

1. Call transaction **LC10 · liveCache: Monitoring · Current Status · Memory Areas · Caches**.

2. Check the liveCache's cache hit ratio and the number of disk accesses. The hit rate should not fall below 99.8%. The number of read accesses since the liveCache was restarted is counted. It can be evaluated only over this period of time, and only with the help of your experience. The number of read accesses to the hard disk should be around zero. Write accesses, on the other hand, give you an impression of the necessary activities when writing a savepoint. The number of write accesses is in no way indicative of a cache's being too small.

Background

The necessary size of the cache areas will increase as the planning data grows. The size of a demand planning version can be determined using transaction **/SAPAPO/OM16** (see Chapter 7). You should check the amount of memory needed by the cache regularly—at least once a week—and in particular after transferring data. The performance of the liveCache depends to a great extent on the utilization of fast cache access. If there is no more room in the cache for all the necessary data, displacements occur and much slower hard disk accesses are required to read all the necessary data. The user will notice the resulting loss in performance immediately.

Solution

Should the cache areas turn out to be too small, they must be extended.

1. Check to see if the liveCache server will allow for an increase in cache size. You should note that in Windows 32-bit systems without AWE, the maximum available cache size for a process is limited to 3 Gb.

2. Select transaction **LC10 · liveCache: Monitoring · Current status · Memory areas · Caches**.

3. On the operating system level, call DBMGUI or select transaction **LC10 · liveCache: Monitoring · Administration · Configuration · Parameter**.

4. Increase the cache parameter CACHE_SIZE.

5. The liveCache must be restarted for the new parameter to come into effect. Consult with the users before you do this!

If the restart fails after you have increased the cache parameter, check the system messages or error messages by selecting transaction **LC10** or DBMGUI. The cause of the failed restart is most likely that there is not enough cache available to cover the needs of the increased parameter. The easiest way to check this is to look at the messages in the *knldiag* file. If this is the case, you will find entries similar to those in List 5.1. In this case, you should lower the parameter again and try to restart once more.

If it is necessary to increase the cache areas, you should also check to see whether there is enough hard disk memory space available for the live-Cache.

Shortage of Memory Space in the Data Devspaces

Symptom
The liveCache's performance is very poor, possibly even resulting in downtime.

Analysis
Call transaction **LC10**, and select **Current status · Memory areas · Devspaces**. Of particular interest are the total size, the permanently occupied memory area, and possibly the temporarily occupied memory area and the free memory area. Temporary memory area should be used only rarely. Memory area may be needed temporarily for executing SQL commands, if larger sort actions are necessary; in the liveCache environment, however, SQL commands are used only in exceptional cases.

If the fill level of the data area exceeds 90% and less than 300 Mb are still available, then a critical situation has been reached.

Background
If the space available in the data devspaces falls below the cited threshold values, writing the next savepoint (checkpoint in liveCache 7.2) may fail. If the data devspaces are completely full, the liveCache is no longer operational. The result is downtime—a particularly critical situation for production operation. Increased requirement of memory area is always caused by a growth in data. This growth is always noticed first in the cache sizes needed and can, in the worst case, lower performance. A shortage of space on disk areas may possibly be overlooked as a result.

When enlarging, you should check the I/O buffer cache area of the live-Cache and the fill level of the hard disk areas. The data devspaces should be around four times bigger than the I/O buffer cache, in total. If you are using liveCache 7.2, the data devspaces should be around eight times bigger than the data cache.

Solution
Extend the disk areas. You can do this by adding an extra file or possibly a new raw device to the data area of the liveCache. In Unix systems, please look out for the necessary authorizations of the user *<liveCache-Name>adm*. The authorization is usually 660, that is, *− rw − rw − r −*.

The actual extension of the data area is done with the liveCache in regular operation. This procedure has hardly any noticeable effect on performance. Proceed as follows:

1. In the APO system, call transaction **LC10**.
2. Branch to the area of **Administration · Devspaces**. Check to see if the liveCache can be extended. You will find the current number of data areas in the field **Size of data area**. In the area **Data area extendibility** in the **to** field you will find the current upper limit. The upper limit must be at least as big again as the current number of devspaces. It is given using the parameter MAXDEVSPACES.
3. If the current number of devspaces is less than the current upper limit, select **Add devspace**. An input window appears, with a suggested name for the new data area.
4. Add the desired size of the new data area.
5. Confirm your entry.

On the liveCache operating system level you can observe the procedure as follows:

```
x_cons <liveCache-Name> sh io <Number Seconds>
```

This command shows you all read and write processes on the disk areas. The display is updated in accordance with <Number Seconds>. If you add a new disk area, you will also be able to see this in the display. For a period of time an increased read and write activity will be discernible in this area.

System Downtime with liveCache 7.4

Symptom
The APO system is started but the users cannot carry out any actions, and they see the hourglass wait symbol.

Analysis

The log area may be full. Check the fill level of the log area using transaction **LC10 · liveCache: Monitoring · Properties**. In the display in Figure 5.9 we see a warning that the log areas are full.

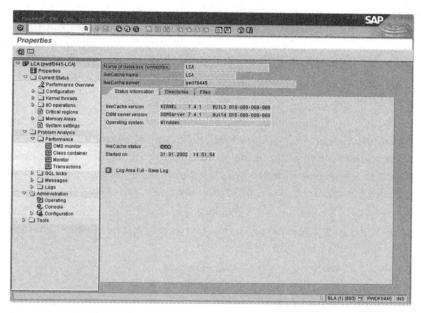

Figure 5.9 liveCache: Monitoring · Properties – Log full

If the alert monitor for the liveCache is activated, this will also report the shortage of space in the log area.

Background

All changes to data in the liveCache are recorded in the log area archive. The log area archive must be backed up regularly so that the backed-up areas can be used again for new data. If the backups have been overlooked or if the archive log area is too small, the log area fills up and no more data can be written. This presents an enormous security risk, so the liveCache stops, and the system shuts down.

Solution

Save the archive log area using the DBMGUI. To avoid the system's shutting down in this manner in the future, you should work with the **AutoLog** option as much as possible. If the archive log still gets too full, check the size and, if necessary, increase the archive log area. You can check the size of the archive log area using transaction **LC10 · liveCache: Monitoring · Current Status · Configuration · Devspaces · Log Devspaces**. An archive log area of 2 Gb should normally suffice. The size of the archive log area needed does not depend on the size of the data area of the liveCache; it depends solely on the volume of data changes. The size should therefore be in correlation with the number of APO system users. If it is necessary to increase the log area, this is done by adding an additional archive devspace in production operation. The procedure is the same as the above-described procedure for adding a data devspace. This procedure has hardly any noticeable effect on performance, either. Proceed as follows:

1. In the APO system, call transaction **LC10**.

2. Branch to the area **liveCache: Monitoring · Configuration · Devspaces**. Check to see if the liveCache can be extended. You will find the current number of data areas in the field **Size of data area**. In the area **Data area extendibility** in the **to** field you will find the current upper limit. The upper limit must be at least as big again as the current number of devspaces. It is set using the parameter MAXARCHIVELOG.

3. If the current number of devspaces is less than the current upper limit, select **Add Log Devspace**. An input window appears with a suggested name for the new data area.

4. Enter the desired size of the new data area.

5. Confirm your entry.

On the liveCache's operating system level you can again observe the procedure as follows:

```
x_cons <liveCache-Name> sh io <Number Seconds>
```

liveCache 7.2   The log area is unlikely to ever' be too small with liveCache 7.2. The log is run in 7.2 as a demo log, so data in the log is automatically overwritten in cycles. Therefore, the log area retains only data that is needed for the possible rollback of an open transaction. As soon as the transaction is completed, the related data is deleted from the log area and this space is once again available. The fill level of the log area fluctuates greatly as a result. You can observe this using transaction **LC10 · liveCache: Monitoring · Current Status · Memory Areas · Log area performance**. Because of this logging mechanism, the log area can be too small only if extremely large transactions are carried out or if a lot of transactions are open at the same time. If there is insufficient space in the logging area, the liveCache system shuts down. In addition, messages are written to *knldiag* (**LC10 · liveCache: Monitoring · Current Status · Problem Analysis · Core**).

If this is the case, you should enlarge the log areas following the same procedure as for extending the data areas. The upper limit for the number of log devspaces is set by the parameter MAXARCHIVELOGS.

Apparent System Downtime with liveCache 7.2

Symptom
The APO system is started but it is not possible to log on, or logging on takes a very long time. Users already logged on cannot carry out any actions, and they see the hourglass wait symbol. The system seems to be down.

Analysis
If you are still logged onto the system, call transaction **LC10**, enter the desired liveCache name, and branch to the **Performance** area. Check to see if the **Checkpoint wanted** option is activated in the **liveCache status** area. If you can no longer execute transaction **LC10**, you must act on the operating system level.

To do so, enter the following:

```
dbmcli -d <liveCache-Name> -n <node> -
u <controluser,passwd> -uSQL sapr3,sap
        sql_execute select * from show_stat_state
        where description='Checkpoint wanted'
```

If the result is Yes, then there is most likely a conflict in writing the checkpoint.

Background
As already explained in the section on the architecture and functions of the liveCache, the checkpoint is a time slot in which information is transferred from the cache to the hard disk areas.

To ensure that data reflects a consistent situation, for a short while no write transactions can be active. To achieve this, once the situation 'Checkpoint wanted' occurs, no new write transactions can be started. Write transactions that have already started can be completed; the system waits until these transactions are finished. Users who wish to start a new write transaction have to wait; for them it seems that the APO system has come to a standstill. Users working with transactions that are still open, on the other hand, do not notice any change in the situation. If the transactions that are still open take a long time, the situation 'Checkpoint wanted' can also last a long time. In normal circumstances the user would not notice any of this. Transactions are generally very short, which, from a technical point of view, means that the delay between two commits is very short. You should note, however, that if transactions are executed in debug mode, no commits are written. In this case, the liveCache must wait for the completion of the debugging procedure before executing the check-point.

You should avoid running transactions in debug mode in production systems!

Solution

Once you have determined that the liveCache has paused in the *'Check-point wanted'* status, proceed as follows:

Start SQL Studio or use DBMCLI to execute the following Select command:

```
Select appl_process, appl_
nodeid, lockmode, process from sysmon_task_
detail s, transactions t where s.dbid = t.process and low
er(t.lockmode) = 'exclusive'
```

The result is a list. In the first column of the list you will see the process number of the work process carrying out write transactions, and in the second column you will see the corresponding server name. This is identified by checking the existing exclusive locks. You should note the work process number and the associated server.

To find out which user and which program is causing the long running transaction, you can also proceed as described below. In any case, the more application servers there are, the bigger drain this method puts on resources:

1. On the operation system level of your application server or your APO DB server, call *dpmon*.
2. From the menu (**m**) select the detailed display of the work process administration table (**l**).
3. Check to see if the application process number determined with DBM-CLI is assigned to a corresponding work process and if it has the status *'Running'*.
4. Resolve the conflict situation. There are two ways to do this:
   ▶ Inform the user by telephone and ask him or her to end the transaction or the debugging procedure.

- ▶ Interrupt the work process—by using the Unix command `kill` or the Task Manager, for example. You can do this without affecting the APO system, because for every terminated work process another is automatically started. Only the transaction is lost, because the assigned work process was resolutely interrupted. You should also observe that when a work process is restarted, the instance profile, and therefore the parameterization of the work process, is read anew. If the profile has changed in the meantime, the work process is started with the new profile.

5. Check to see if the checkpoint has been written. Once again you can use the DBMCLI command described in the analysis. If the conflict situation has been resolved, the liveCache should be in the status 'Checkpoint wanted' No. This is immediately noticeable to the users, who can now continue working. In some circumstances, however, several transactions may hinder the execution of the checkpoint. If the liveCache is still in the status of 'Checkpoint wanted' Yes, you should start from the first step again.

The procedure for resolving this checkpoint conflict situation is described in SAPNet Note 325384.

It should be emphasized once again that the situation described occurs extremely rarely and when it does it is often in connection with debugging procedures. The means of resolving a conflict situation when writing a checkpoint is described here because, although it is a very rare occurrence, it is also a particularly bothersome one. You should always try to avoid debugging in production systems. In development systems you should check to see if the recommended two- to three-hour period for writing checkpoints can be extended. We would also like to point out that long-running background jobs are not the same as a long-running transaction. The length of a transaction is delimited by a commit. Long-running jobs generally consist of many individual transactions. They do not therefore necessarily hamper the execution of a checkpoint.

The best way to check the regular writing of checkpoints is to use transaction **/SAPAPO/OM11**. There you will find a list of all the important events in the operation of a liveCache. Executed checkpoints are recorded as *CheckPoint* actions. For a more detailed description of the logged events, see Chapter 6.

Another possibility is to check the job for writing checkpoints on the basis of the report program `/SAPAPO/OM_CHECKPOINT_ WRITE`. The recommended name for this job is OM_CHECKPOINT_ WRITE. You can branch to it in the job overview, transaction **SM37**. Limit the display to the job OM_CHECKPOINT_WRITE for writing the checkpoint. The duration of each individual job will let you see how much time is needed to execute the checkpoint.

The time needed to execute the checkpoint depends, of course, on the size of the cache area and on the change activities in the liveCache. You can expect around two minutes, as a general guideline.

Execution times that vary greatly from this indicate conflicts in writing the checkpoint.

 Because of the special characteristics of liveCache 7.2, you should at all costs try to avoid totally stopping the liveCache (kill and so on). This would involve a recovery of the liveCache!

6 LCApps (COM Routines)

Aspects of system administration, and especially the analysis tools for LCApps, are of particular interest to operators of APO systems.

COM routines, now called *LCApps*, represent one of the most important advances in the development of APO software. We have already referred in Chapter 2 to the role of LCApps or COM routines in data processing. So far, only SAP uses the technology behind LCApps in conjunction with the liveCache. However, in the future, other SAP software products will also be equipped with this technology.

COM routines are fundamentally different from the data processing with SQL commands which has been used so far. SQL commands are processed to read data from tables or to change it. The business process logic is accomplished with ABAP. COM routines, on the other hand, are C++ programs that are linked directly with the core of the liveCache (dynamically linked). The business process logic is contained in the COM routine in question. From an ABAP point of view, calling a COM routine is like calling a stored procedure. As a result, it is more difficult to analyze a business process. If you try to analyze a process flow based on coding, the procedures remain concealed in the COM routines; only input and output parameters can be identified. Which COM routine handles which business process has not yet been documented by SAP AG. COM routines are used not only for transferring business processes, however, but for the administration of the liveCache as well.

6.1 Number and Version

The number of COM routines depends on the liveCache version and the APO release used. You will find the files *sap*.dll* and *sap*.lst* in the directory */sapdb/<liveCache SID>/db/sap*. The *sap*.dll* files are the libraries in which the COM routines are collected. COM routines that belong to an application module are also combined in a DLL. The corresponding *sap*.lst* files also contain a list of all available COM routines. The number of COM routines is around 300, but it grows continuously. You can use transaction **/SAPAPO/OM04** in your APO system to determine the version of the COM routines. For every DLL, and as such, for every application module, the release, patch, and change list, along with the date of the last change and the size of the DLL file, are displayed. You should make sure that the releases of COM routines, the liveCache and other support packages are consistent, especially if you are implementing APO support packages. Information on this is published in the relevant Notes.

6.2 Transactional Simulations

An important feature of liveCache technology is the formation of consistent views, or transactional simulations, as described in Chapter 4. Each APO system user can create and use such transactional simulations during his or her work. The data processed by the COM routines is stored in the OMS data cache and in the OMS heap; transactional simulations are automatically removed from the OMS heap on completion of the work. However, if the user does not close his or her work—if the user forgets about the simulation, for example—it cannot be automatically deleted by the system. Eventually the OMS is filled with data that it no longer needs. To combat this, the report program /SAPAPO/OM_REORG_ DAILY must be run in background processing every day (see also SAPNet Note 139558). Transactional simulations that are more than 24 hours old should be deleted. You can get an overview of how many transactional simulations are in liveCache OMS using transaction **LC10 · liveCache: Monitoring · Problem Analysis · Performance · Monitor · OMS Versions** (see Figure 6.1).

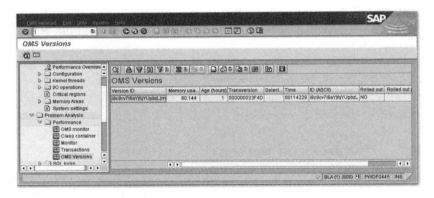

Figure 6.1 Overview of transactional simulations

Another important background job is the report program /SAPAPO/OM_ DELETE_OLD_SIMSESS. This report ensures that transactional simulations which could not be removed normally, due to an unexpected termination of an APO transaction, are deleted from the liveCache. This report should be scheduled to run every half hour in the APO system.

APO 3.0 For APO release 3.0, this report program is supplied with support package 20.

6.3 Performance Trace

When using COM routines, the performance trace (previously called *SQL trace*) in APO systems looks different from the structure with which you are familiar. It can be activated via **System · Services · Performance Trace**. Whereas in R/3 systems only SQL statements were recorded, in APO systems COM routines are initiated via the SQL interface and are also recorded. For COM routines, however, some columns in the log can be interpreted differently. The following descriptions of the SQL trace apply from patch 520 of the database interface library for the liveCache (*dbadaslib*) of R/3 kernel 4.6D. Table 6.1 shows an extract from a performance trace, which contains calls from liveCache COM routines.

Checking the entry in the column **Con** (connection) is the quickest way to identify the calling of COM routines. Either LCA or LCD is noted there, depending on the connection used to address the liveCache. COM routines are executed in the liveCache in several steps, which can be reproduced in the SQL trace. When a COM routine is executed for the first time, it is not yet in the statement cache of the liveCache memory. In the first step, therefore, it is "prepared", which is comparable to parsing an SQL statement. In the performance trace we can recognize this step by the action PREPARE in the column **Oper** (Operation). If the parsed COM routine is still in the statement cache, however, parsing is not necessary. The next step is the operation REEXEC, which marks the actual start of execution of the COM routine. The column **Statements** mirrors the calling up of a COM routine with CALL USER and the name of the COM routine. As with SQL statements, the program that prompted the calling of the COM routine is displayed in the column **Program**. Similarly, the name of the COM routine called is also given in the column **Objectname**. The parameter with which the COM routine works is presented as ?. By double-clicking on the command, the parameter is shown in greater detail. List 6.1 shows an extract from the parameter list of the COM routine SAPAPO_PP_ORDER_GET_DATA. Transferred single values are displayed directly. Unfortunately, this is not possible for internal tables.

hh:mm:ss.ms	Duration	Program	Objectname	Oper	Curs	Array	Rec	RC	Con	Statements
12:55:46.847	4.411	/SAPAPO/SAPLOM_PLANNING	"SAPAPO_PP_ ORDER_ CHANGE"	REEXEC	2007	1	0	0	LCA	"SAPAPO_PP_ORDER_CHANGE"
12:55:46.852	24	/SAPAPO/SAPLOM_PLANNING	"SAPAPO_PP_ ORDER_ CHANGE"	EXECSTA			2	100	LCA	FETCH from ABAP internal table (2)
12:55:46.852	844	/SAPAPO/SAPLOM_PLANNING	"SAPAPO_PP_ ORDER_ CHANGE"	EXECSTA		1	0	0	LCA	DBPROC continuing …
										………
12:55:49.359	1.251	/SAPAPO/SAPLOPT_LB	/SAPAPO/OPTUSR	OPEN	101		0	0	R/3	SELECT WHERE "OPTID" = 'DPS01' /*Y8A00000198B5UG5903iSAPAPOiSAPLOPTwL ………
12:55:45.360	282	/SAPAPO/SAPLOPT_LB	/SAPAPO/OPTUSR	FETCH	101	1	1	0	R/3	
12:55:45.720	127	/SAPAPO/SAPLOM_PLANNING	"SAPAPO_PP_ ORDER_ GET_DATA"	PREPARE					LCA	CALL USER".SAPAPO_PP_ORDER_GET_DATA" (?, ?, ?, ?, ?
12:55:46.881	4.152	/SAPAPO/SAPLOM_PLANNING	"SAPAPO_PP_ ORDER_ GET_DATA"	REEXEC	2002	1	0	0	LCA	CALL USER".SAPAPO_PP_ORDER_GET_DATA" (?, ?, ?, ?, ?
12:55:46.885	22	/SAPAPO/SAPLOM_PLANNING	"SAPAPO_PP_ ORDER_ GET_DATA"	EXECSTA			1	100	LCA	FETCH from ABAP internal table (1)
…		/SAPAPO/SAPLOM_PLANNING	"SAPAPO_PP_ ORDER_ GET_DATA"	EXECSTA			0	0	LCA	DBPROC continuing …
		/SAPAPO/SAPLOM_PLANNING	"SAPAPO_PP_ ORDER_ GET_DATA"	EXECSTA			1	0	LCA	INSERT into ABAP internal table (19)
		/SAPAPO/SAPLOM_PLANNING	"SAPAPO_PP_ ORDER_ GET_DATA"	EXECSTA			0	0	LCA	DBPROC continuing …
		/SAPAPO/SAPLOM_PLANNING	"SAPAPO_PP_ ORDER_ GET_DATA"	EXECSTA			1	0	LCA	INSERT into ABAP internal table (10)
		/SAPAPO/SAPLOM_PLANNING	"SAPAPO_PP_ ORDER_ GET_DATA"	EXECSTA			0	0	LCA	DBPROC continuing …

Table 6.1 Extract from a performance trace with COM routines

```
SQL Statement
CALL USER".SAPAPO_PP_ORDER_GET_
DATA" ( ?, ?, ?, ?, ?, ?, ?, ?, ?, ?, ?, ?, ?, ?,
?, ?, ?, ?, ?, ?, ?, ?, ?, ?, ? )
Variables
A0(CH,61) = TEST_TSIM_01_WILLXXXXXWILL          000000
A1(CH,8)  = ########
A2(CH,21) = <ABAP internal table>
A3(CH,21) = <ABAP internal table>
A4(CH,21) =   X   XXXX        XXX
A5(CH,21) = <ABAP internal table>
A6(CH,21) = <ABAP internal table>
A7(CH,21) = <ABAP internal table>
A8(CH,21) = <ABAP internal table>
 . . .
```

Listing 6.1 Parameters of a COM routine

The following phases in the execution of a COM routine are all identified by the operation EXECSTA. In the **Statement** column we find:

▶ FETCH from ABAP internal table (x)
The COM routine is transferred as a parameter of an internal table. The internal tables transferred as parameters are numbered again, starting at zero. Fetch shows that in this step the x-th of the tables transferred as parameters is read. The number of rows transferred is recorded in the column **Rec**. For large internal tables the transfer can also be done in several steps. The largest block that can be transferred is 20 Kb. The table is fully transferred only if 100 is given as the return code in the column **RC**.

▶ INSERT into ABAP internal table (x)
If the results of the COM routine are given via an internal table, this is marked by this entry in the column **Statements**. Here too, the number of the parameter in question is given in parenthesis.

▶ DBPROC continuing . . .
If a COM routine is processing, this is indicated with this entry.

The processing of a COM routine is closed only when the next COM routine or an SQL statement is called. The overall runtime of a COM routine is calculated from the sum of the runtimes of its individual steps. Please note that much like the SQL statements, this runtime includes some network time if the liveCache is not located on the same server as the APO instance.

6.4 COM Trace

A special COM trace can be activated for COM routines. However, please note that this trace should be used only after consulting with SAP support. The know-how of the COM developers is required to analyze this trace. In addition, activating the COM trace leads to a loss of performance. In this book, therefore, we will show only how the trace can be activated in case of emergency and how to obtain SAP support for analysis.

The COM trace is written to the operating system of the liveCache in the form of *.txt* files. These files are located in the */sapdb/data/wrk/<liveCache SID>* directory. Naming follows the model *lcapo_com_trace_<number>.txt*. Should errors occur in the execution of COM routines, these are logged in the file, regardless of whether the COM trace is activated or not. You can activate a detailed logging of the execution of COM routines using transaction **/SAPAPO/OM02** (see Figure 6.2). In the **Trace File No.** area you can set, among other things, the number and size of the trace files. If the option **Cyclical Trace File** is activated, the file is overwritten, starting at the beginning, as soon as the defined size is reached. If a particular situation is to be recorded, the COM trace should be written to an explicitly selected file. If the file is already being used by earlier trace records, it can be initialized and cleaned before starting a new recording.

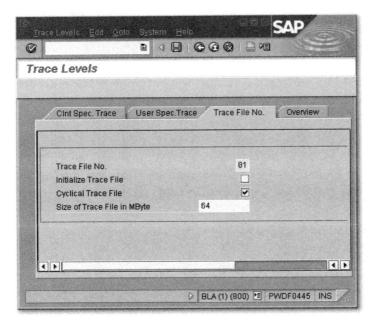

Figure 6.2 Settings for the COM trace file

Since COM routines can process very complex procedures, the trace should be restricted to what is absolutely necessary. The COM trace can be specifically activated for a certain client, user, and COM routine. Independently of this, the trace can be activated for application-specific COM routine groups such as pegging, RPM (*Rapid Planning Matrix*), or resources. Figure 6.3 shows client-specific customizing for the COM trace.

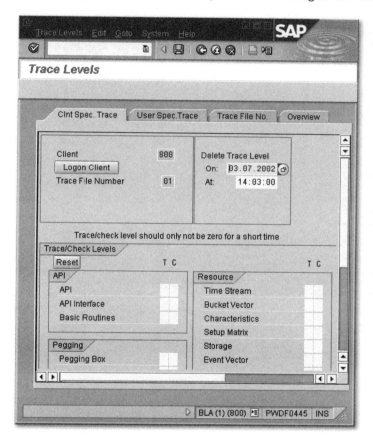

Figure 6.3 Activating the COM trace

A trace level can be set for each selected application and its COM routines. At level 0, or if no level is entered, only errors are recorded. For more detailed recordings, you can raise the trace level as high as 9. To do this you make entries in column **T**.

Use transaction **/SAPAPO/OM01** to display the COM trace. In the initial screen (see Figure 6.4) the current trace file can be selected using the defined number. If the current trace file is unknown, you can use input help for the **Number of Trace File** field. All available trace files, together with details on when they were last accessed, are displayed. In addition, you can use the copy of the current trace file to create a backup copy of the trace in any other file. You can also delimit the area to be copied. List 6.2 shows the contents of a COM trace, as it is always written at level 0 for errors.

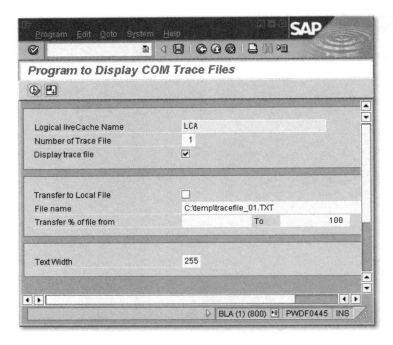

Figure 6.4 Display of a COM trace

```
- - - - - - - - - - - - - - - - - - - - - - - - - - - - - - - - - - - - - - - - - -
|Type|Message text                                              |Ltxt|
- - - - - - - - - - - - - - - - - - - - - - - - - - - - - - - - - - - - - - - - - -
|    |Source system: LPOCLNT800 User: GG083                     |    |
|    |Transaction: CM10 Function module:                        |    |
|    |/SAPAPO/CIF_ORDER_INBOUND                                 |    |
|    |Ordertype 6 OrderNo 000001090979                          |    |
|    |Error occurred                                            |    |
|    |=============== Error-start ===============               |    |
|    |Ordertype 6 OrderNo 000001090979                          |    |
|    |Production order 1090979 (in-house), Source -             |    |
|    |of supply                                                 |    |
|    |Error in an activity of the operation                     |    |
```

```
|   |Error in COM routines-Call using          |   |
|   |Application program (Return-Code 17929)    |   |
|   |----------------End of error---------------|   |
|   |Error occurred                             |   |
```

Listing 6.2 Extract of a COM trace

List 6.2 shows the log of an error that occurred in the execution of the
COM routine /SAPAPO/CIF_ORDER_INBOUND. The COM routine was
terminated by error 17929. You can use transaction **/SAPAPO/OM10** to
display the related error text.

6.5 Self Test

You can carry out a general test of the COM routines using report
/SAPAPO/OM_LCCHECK. At the report runtime, a test environment is created for most COM routines using the data already available in the live-
Cache, then the COM routines are run, and the test data is subsequently
deleted. If the report runs with no errors, we can assume that the COM
routines, the liveCache, the APO DB, and the SAP kernel are correctly and
consistently installed. However, no conclusions can be drawn from the
report program regarding the performance of the liveCache, COM routines, and so on. The test data for this report is generated dynamically and
therefore depends on the content of the liveCache.

6.6 Analyses for the liveCache and COM Routines

Transaction **/SAPAPO/OM13** offers a roundup of the most important
tools for the liveCache and COM objects. The following functions are
available:

▶ **Versions**
Displays the versions (changelist) of the COM routines. Equivalent to
transaction **/SAPAPO/OM04**.

▶ **Checks**
Online tests carried out to check the installation, configuration, and
availability of the liveCache and its COM routines. The *LCA* and *LDA*
connections, the operating mode of the liveCache, and the defined
RFC connections are checked. If COM tracing is activated, then this is
also displayed. A check is also made to see if the maintenance jobs
/SAPAPO/OM_REORG_DAILY and /SAPAPO/OM_DELETE_OLD_SIM-
SESS are scheduled.

▶ **Network**
Permits you to test the network connection to the liveCache using `niping`. The network connection to the liveCache is at least as critical as the connection to the APO DB. A network with a bandwidth of at least 100 Mbits should be used between APO instances and the live-Cache. If the network is not strong enough, the performance gains obtained from using the liveCache rather than normal RDBMS are easily cancelled out. By using the `niping` command you can measure the volume and the transfer rate between the liveCache and the APO instance. The value calculated, `bw2`, should be as close as possible to the bandwidth used between the APO instance and the liveCache. In normal operation, data is transferred between the APO instance and the liveCache in 32-bit blocks. The value `avg` indicates the average time needed to transfer this type of packet to the liveCache and back. Please see SAPNet Notes 447560 and 458221 for information on the installation and usage of the `niping` command.

▶ **Current messages**
Corresponds to the current liveCache messages in the *knldiag* file, which can also be viewed using transaction **LC10 · liveCache: Monitoring · Current status · Properties · Files**.

▶ **Error messages**
Corresponds to the liveCache error messages in the *knldiag.err* file, which can also be viewed using transaction **LC10 · liveCache: Monitoring · Current status · Properties · Files**.

▶ **Initialization**
The liveCache's initialization log. It can also be viewed using transaction **LC10**.

▶ **Logging**
All important administrative actions for the liveCache are displayed, similar to when using transaction **/SAPAPO/OM11**.

7 Backup and Recovery

In this chapter we will explain the differences between backup and recovery in an APO system as opposed to an R/3 system. Because the systems are closely linked, it is very important that consistency is maintained through the entire system landscape in the event of a recovery.

7.1 Components, System, and System Landscape

When an APO system is introduced to a system landscape, or even beforehand, the individual systems are closely linked to each other in a system landscape. If just one system fails, this affects the functioning of the entire system landscape. The reliability of a single system therefore affects the availability of the system landscape. The system landscape can be said to be reliable only if each individual system is reliable. Therefore, you need to be able to guarantee the same level of dependability for each system in the landscape. A decisive factor in determining the necessary level of reliability is the demands made by the business process. System administrators and relevant departments must work together to find the optimal variant, taking cost and usage into consideration.

We will assume that you are familiar with the options for increasing the reliability of R/3 systems. In this chapter we will focus on the technical possibilities for ensuring the APO system's high availability. Just as the reliability of the system landscape is determined by the weakest system, the reliability of an individual system is determined by the reliability of its weakest component. The APO system is made up of various components that are partially independent. The APO DB and the liveCache are two particularly important components. If the APO DB goes down, the APO system goes down. Should the liveCache crash, the APO system instance would still be available, but its functionality would be limited so severely that it would be tantamount to a complete failure of the APO system. On the other hand, if the cost-based optimizers of the APO system fail, this affects only the business processes that use the optimizers. These are usually tasks like planning steps or planning runs. You must therefore check to see how important optimizers are for a business process. It may also be necessary to find a high-availability solution for them.

In general, then, the question of APO system's availability is reduced to a question of the availability of the APO DB and the liveCache. Nevertheless, the connections between components and the systems should not be neglected.

High availability If you need a high-availability solution for your APO system, you must secure both the APO DB and the liveCache. The APO DB is based on the RDBMS, with which you are familiar from R/3 systems. As a result, the usual techniques for high-availability or hot-standby databases can be implemented. For the liveCache we should differentiate between releases 7.2 and 7.4. liveCache 7.2 does not support the well-known high-availability or hot-standby solutions. You cannot implement an automatic switch, especially when using with the Demand Planning module, and some manual reworking is always necessary. liveCache 7.4, on the other hand, works in the same way as familiar RDBMS. As a result, high-availability and hot-standby solutions are fully applicable.

Strategy One of the most important aspects of availability is the backup and recovery strategy for the APO system.

In detail, backup and recovery in the APO system involve:

▶ Backup and recovery of the APO DB

▶ Backup and recovery of the liveCache

▶ Restoration of consistency between the APO DB and the liveCache

▶ Restoration of consistency between the APO system and dedicated systems

These components must be restored based on whether only one component or the entire APO system is affected. For example, if a complete recovery cannot be achieved, it may be necessary to establish consistency between the components, the APO system, and the landscape separately. Consistency of the APO system within the system landscape must also be preserved or re-established. A recovery of the APO system and its dedicated systems cannot be dealt with as an isolated event, ignoring the links between the systems. You will need to start to reconstruct the system by working first on the components that have gone down and then work step by step until finally the entire system landscape has been repaired—that is, you work from the bottom up. Overall, backup and recovery in an APO system is much more complex than in an R/3 system that has no interfaces to other systems.

7.2   Data Security of the APO DB

The APO DB is the part of the APO system that is most like R/3. All techniques and methods to increase data security, including backup and recovery, that you know from R/3 can be transferred to the APO DB. You can also use the database-specific tools in the usual way for backup and recovery in the APO DB. If for some reason you are still unable to carry out a complete recovery of the APO DB, data will be lost as a result and consistency between the liveCache and the dedicated systems will have to be re-established. The consistency checks available are described in Chapter 8. It is strongly recommended that you avoid loss of data in the APO DB by using an appropriate backup plan.

7.3   Data Security of the liveCache

In the event of a loss of liveCache content, not all data contained in the liveCache can be recreated from the APO DB or the dedicated systems by running an initialization. The liveCache requires a backup and recovery strategy of its own. In this respect, the liveCache since version 7.4 works in the same way as an RDBMS. Therefore, complete liveCache backups and log backups are needed. The basic principles and tools available for this are presented below.

7.3.1   Backup Strategy

When working out a backup and recovery strategy for an APO system, you must answer questions about how often the complete backup or backups of the components should be carried out. Factors of cost will influence your answers to these questions in addition to considerations of data security. In any case, data security and thus the backup and recovery strategies for the APO DB and the liveCache should be similar.

One question is how often a complete backup should be run. The answer is: the more often a complete backup is run, the better. It is always quicker to run a restore of a backup than to recover numerous log backups after the restore. How frequently you need to run backups is directly related to how frequently changes are made to data. Since the liveCache is often only a few Gbytes in size, a complete backup represents a low load. As a result, you can carry out a backup for the liveCache very quickly. A basic recommendation would be to run a daily backup of the liveCache and a regular backup of the archive log, depending on the log. The *AutoLog* mode should be used when possible. Backups should be maintained for at least four weeks.

Another question is whether or not it is necessary to stop the APO DB and the liveCache for a backup. If you stop the APO DB and the liveCache to carry out a backup, you will get a consistent backup of the two components, at a precise point in time. You will not even need any further log backups to create this consistency. If, on the other hand, you run a backup while the APO system is operative, then in the event of a recovery, you would achieve consistency only after the restore has been completed and the logs recreated. It is not possible to achieve total consistency between the APO DB and the liveCache until the entire recovery procedure has been completed. Admittedly, it is open to discussion how such a situation was ever even practical in the APO system. To avoid loss of data, you would follow the log backups up to the current point in time anyway. A consistent complete backup of the APO system in *offline* mode would make sense only if the APO system were to be copied. This type of backup would also make sense if it meant that you could preserve a situation in the APO system to which the system could be returned if necessary. This could be the case, for example, after the initial data load or before an upgrade. It is hard to imagine any other useful applications for backups in the *offline* mode. In fact, this type of backup would hamper normal APO operation.

 Offline backups should, in any event, be done with the help of the liveCache or APO DB tools and should not be done by copying files. If you use the latter method there is no guarantee of the consistency of the files and, in particular, the data contained in them.

7.3.2 Backup of liveCache 7.4

Carrying out a backup for liveCache 7.4 is essentially no different from a backup of the APO DB based on a RDBMS. The liveCache tools necessary for this were presented in Chapter 5.

You should be familiar with transaction **DB13** from R/3 systems. It can be used to schedule backups and other administrative actions for R/3 DB maintenance to run in the background. In APO release 3.1, this *weekly planning*, as it is known, is supported only for the APO DB. The possibility of scheduling backup jobs for the liveCache, for example, is planned only for the next release of APO. However, you can still plan backups of the liveCache by executing the corresponding DBMCLI commands as external commands in background jobs.

7.3.3 Logging in liveCache 7.4

liveCache release 7.4 offers complete physical logging for all changes made to data in caches. Only data in the private OMS heap is excluded from this. The logging comparable to logging in RDMBS, and we will therefore assume that you are familiar with the procedure. There are differences in some technical details, but these have only a slight effect on the administrative requirements. Due to the extremely high demands on liveCache performance, analogous requirements are made on the I/O volume in the archive log devspaces. Performance problems when writing to the archive log area could have a negative effect, particularly at times such as planning runs, when a lot of changes are being made to data.

So far, the liveCache has been operated in the *Single* log mode. This means that each change is saved once on the log devspaces. Log mode is determined by the liveCache parameter LOGMODE. The parameter can be checked using transaction **LC10** or DBMGUI or DBMCLI.

As in RDBMS, archive log devspaces are the liveCache memory areas with the highest input and output activity. Given that the data volume for the archive log devspaces is so critical, these devspaces, more so than log areas in RDBMS, should not be operated in RAID5 disk areas of the hardware. Due to technical calculations when writing data, RAID5 is demonstrably, and in log areas obviously, slower than RAID1 systems (for example). This can also be said of storage systems, in principle, but in this case the technology usually cancels out the loss in performance. Storage systems work with relatively high memory and increased reliability, compared with simple RAID5, thanks to special controller technology. However, if the resulting write load on the disk is greater than can be temporarily stored in the disk memory, a significant loss of performance will also occur with storage systems. However, it is difficult to foresee which conditions in APO operation could lead to such a load. It is therefore advisable to test the planned productive load beforehand, as realistically as possible. If I/O bottlenecks occur, storage systems should be configured in such a way that the areas of the archive log devspaces are operated in RAID1. If necessary, the disk memory can also be upgraded.

Details on storage systems and their characteristics should be discussed with the hardware producer.

Backups of the archive log devspaces are done with the corresponding functions in the DBMGUI, but they can also be automated with the help of DBMCLI commands. It is not yet possible to use weekly planning in the

APO system (transaction **DB13**) for backups of the liveCache, but corresponding DBMCLI commands can be planned with CRON or similar Windows technology. As you know from RDBMS, if the log areas get full, the situation would be critical for the liveCache, and the liveCache would crash. You must therefore pay particular attention to creating regular backups of the liveCache log. To make this easier, the liveCache offers you the option of activating the *AutoLog* mode. This can be done from DBMGUI using **Backup • AutoLog on/off**. You can also check to see if the *AutoLog* option is set or not using the DBMCKI command `autosave_show`. When activating the *AutoLog* option, a medium—which must be a file name on the hard disk—must be allocated. A consecutive number is automatically added to the selected file name on each consecutive log backup. In the *AutoLog* mode, there will automatically be a log backup to the assigned medium as soon as a log segment is filled (see Chapter 5).

 Use the *AutoLog* option to automatically backup the content of the log. This is the safest and simplest way to avoid the log's becoming too full.

7.3.4 Logging in liveCache 7.2

The change from release 7.2 to 7.4 has been like a quantum leap. In release 7.2, delivered with APO 3.0, there was no actual physical logging; instead, a logical logging was executed with SQL methods. When APO systems were originally developed it was assumed that the liveCache would require no logging, and that it would be possible to restore all data from the APO DB or the dedicated systems as quickly as possible. This assumption turned out to be false. The APO system was used in such a comprehensive way that the liveCache exceeded the originally expected dimensions. It simply took too long to completely restore the data in the liveCache. As a result, it was not long before new, special logging was developed. As a result, the administration and the functions of logging of releases 7.2 and 7.4 are fundamentally different. Since liveCache release 7.2 is still widely used, we will now present the logging and the associated backup and recovery for it.

In release 7.2, logging works on a logical level. Unfortunately, this does not cover all objects in the APO application module; changes to data from the area of Demand Planning (DP) are not recorded. Similarly, changes to inactive planning versions and some automotive-specific data is not included in this logging either. This data must be repaired with special tools.

The very brave can completely renounce logging. We would insist in pointing out, however, that in the event of a crash, some data would always be lost. You would have to re-initialize the liveCache, and transaction data would have to be reloaded from the dedicated systems—in other words, you would need to do an initial load. All in all, this is not an acceptable solution.

Logging in 7.2 comprises several different techniques, which we shall now discuss.

Checkpoint

To be precise, this is not a logging method as such. Rather, what is referred to as a *checkpoint* is written at a pre-defined frequency. This means that all changes that are originally made only in the cache area of the liveCache, are saved to the hard disk area of the liveCache.

You can initiate the checkpoint by executing the report program /SAPAPO/OM_CHECKPOINT_WRITE in the background in the APO system. With appropriate parameters, this report program also allows for the execution of other actions, which will be described below in the relevant place.

One important question to ask when configuring the checkpoint is, how often should checkpoints be written? On one hand, the checkpoint can slow down work in the APO system; on the other hand, the checkpoint greatly increases data security. As a result, it is advisable to initiate checkpoints as often as possible for the sake of data security. In particular, if you are using DP that is not collected from the actual logging, you should allow checkpoints to be written every two to three hours. Should critically long-running transactions develop, such as planning runs, the report program /SAPAPO/OM_CHECKPOINT_WRITE can also be scheduled as an immediately following jobstep or one controlled by events. In the event of a checkpoint conflict, as described in Chapter 5, you can use the liveCache parameter REQUEST_TIMEOUT. This parameter defines, in seconds, how long the system should wait for a requested lock. Once this time be exceeded, the action—in this case, a checkpoint—is terminated.

Synchronous Logging

Synchronous logging of the liveCache is particularly important in the event of a recovery after a crash situation. Logging for liveCache version 7.2 is defined with the help of transaction **/SAPAPO/OM06**. The settings made are client-dependent. They apply to the client on which the settings are made.

With synchronous logging, in addition to the regular checkpoint, every change in the liveCache, except for changes to DP data, is recorded in the APO DB. Recording means that the change made to the data is reproduced in four tables in the APO DB. This logging should by no means be compared with writing a log in the Archive Log Areas, with which you are familiar from RDBMS or liveCache 7.4. Synchronous logging in liveCache 7.2 is a specific procedure that works at object level. Two log areas exist for this in the APO DB, known as *log areas* A and B. One log area is in turn made up of four tables in which changes to the relevant objects are saved. In log area A the tables are called:

▶ */sapapo/lc_logha*
  For order headers

▶ */sapapo/lc_logca*
  Cluster table for order data

▶ */sapapo/lc_logfa*
  For fixed pegging relationships

▶ */sapapo/lc_logsa*
  For the key of the modified master data

The tables in the second log area, B, differ from those in log area A only in their names. Instead of the *a* at the end of the name, there is a *b*, such as */sapapo/lc_loghb*. The log area is changed after each checkpoint and the data in the "old" log area is deleted. The active log area in each case contains the changes to the data since the last checkpoint.

Archive log area You can also activate an archive log area. To do so, start transaction **/SAPAPO/OM06** and select the option **Archive log data**. The archive log area is in turn made up of four tables in the APO DB. These tables are named in line with the tables in log areas A and B:

▶ */sapapo/lc_loghz*

▶ */sapapo/lc_logcz*

- ▶ /sapapo/lc_logfz
- ▶ /sapapo/lc_logsz

After each checkpoint, the content of the currently inactive log area is copied to the archive log area. Data already in the archive log area is not overwritten; instead, the new data is entered in the table. As a result, the tables in the archive log area are continuously growing. You can learn the current size of the tables in the archive log area using transaction **DB02** or **CCMS · Control/Monitoring · Performance menu · Database · Tables/Indexes**.

To delete the contents of the archive log area, it is best to use the corresponding option in report program `/SAPAPO/OM_ CHECKPOINT_WRITE`. We recommend that you delete the archive log area only if you have previously been able to successfully backup the liveCache using an option of this same report. The log area should be deleted approximately every 24 hours. To delete the contents of the archive log area again, the report program `/SAPAPO/OM_ARCHIVE_LOGAREA_DEL` is used internally.

The length of time needed to execute a checkpoint increases when the archive log area is activated because on each checkpoint, data is copied from the then-inactive log area to the archive log area. How long this process takes depends, largely, on the data volume to be copied.

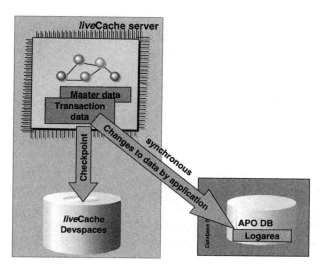

Figure 7.1 Synchronous logging in liveCache 7.2

Figure 7.1 shows how data is dealt with in synchronous logging. Because the logging data is transferred to the APO DB, it is critical to performance that the network connection be fast enough. Problems with the network would be ruinous.

7.3.5 Backup of liveCache 7.2

Because of the different technology, backup of liveCache release 7.2 is also linked with the report program /SAPAPO/OM_CHECKPOINT_WRITE. Whereas with release 7.4, the DBMGUI is enough for a backup, in release 7.2 a checkpoint must first be written and logging must be activated. As a result, a backup can be initiated only with the help of the job /SAPAPO/OM_CHECKPOINT_WRITE. Backups that are executed with only the DBMGUI misrepresent the logging within the APO system. This procedure is likely to lead to inconsistencies.

Figure 7.2 shows the possibilities of variant configuration for report program /SAPAPO/OM_CHECKPOINT_WRITE.

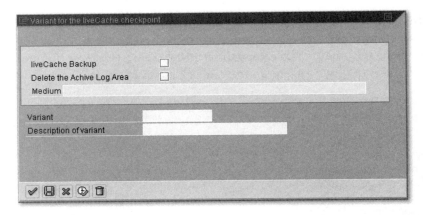

Figure 7.2 Variant configuration of the report program /SAPAPO/OM_CHECKPOINT_WRITE

Check the corresponding box if a backup should be carried out in the course of the checkpoint. Select a medium which you have previously defined with the help of the DBMGUI, as described in Chapter 5. The archive log area can be deleted simultaneously by selecting the corresponding option. However, this option is effective only if you have been able to successfully complete the backup.

7.3.6 History of the liveCache

Since APO version 3.0 from Support Package 10, all important events in the operation of the liveCache are logged. This log can be accessed using transaction **/SAPAPO/OM11**.

Figure 7.3 gives an example of how this type of log may look. In this case, we have a log of a liveCache 7.2. With release 7.4, actions related to the checkpoint do not apply.

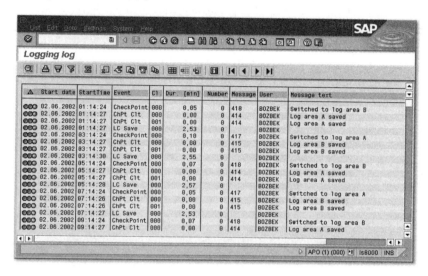

Figure 7.3 Extract from the log table

The logged action's return code is indicated in the first column with a traffic light symbol. The duration of an action, the user who started the action, the return code of the action, and the corresponding message are also displayed. The **Number** column is relevant only for the actions *ChPt Clt (live-Cache 7.2)* and *Recovery*.

In release 7.2, the value in the column **Number** reflects the number of rows in log table (order headers) */sapapo/logha* or */sapapo/loghb*. Should the liveCache crash, and a recovery is required, followed by a roll forward using the records in the log area, the duration of this roll forward depends greatly on the number of records in the log area. You can assume that 100,000 to 150,000 records would take roughly half an hour. Of course, this estimate is strongly influenced by the underlying hardware and the network. Nevertheless, this rule can be used as a rough estimate to calculate, for example, whether the checkpoint described is run often enough. The recovery time needed for the liveCache is the sum of the time

liveCache 7.2

needed to restore the liveCache backup plus the time needed to recover the records in the log area. The time needed to restore the liveCache backup will be around the same as was needed for creating the backup. Recovering the records in the log area also requires *#records / 150,000 * 0.5 h*. If the recovery time estimated in this way does not meet expectations, checkpoints should be written more frequently. Depending on the log mode and the option selected, report program `/SAPAPO/OM_ CHECKPOINT_WRITE` can carry out more actions than are found in log /SAPAPO/OM11. In any case, the job always triggers the action *CheckPoint* to write the liveCache checkpoint. This action should always take around the same length of time. Time variations are usually due to different levels of change activity by APO users, but may also indicate problems with writing the checkpoint (see Chapter 5). Table 7.1 shows the events that are logged.

Event	Meaning	Client dependent?
Init	The liveCache is initialized.	No
LogChange (liveCache 7.2)	The logging mode is changed. A logging mode always applies to only the current client.	Yes
IC Save (liveCache 7.2)	The liveCache is saved using the report /sapao/om_checkpoint_write and the relevant options.	No
CheckPoint (liveCache 7.2)	A checkpoint is written with the help of report /sapapo/om_checkpoint_write. In the course of this checkpoint, there is a switch to the other log area. The message text gives information on which log area then becomes active.	No
ChPt Clt (liveCache 7.2)	The active log area is stored in the archive log area.	No
ArchADel (liveCache 7.2)	The archive log area is deleted.	No
Recovery	A recovery of the liveCache is executed.	No

Table 7.1 Logged events

All records in this log can be deleted with the transaction **/SAPAPO/OM12**.

7.4 Recovery

Of the events that make a recovery necessary, we can differentiate between hardware problems and software or logical problems. Here we will discuss *point-in-time recovery* in relation to logical problems.

7.4.1 Point-in-Time Recovery

By point-in-time recovery we refer to the recovery of a system not up to the current time, but only up to some point in the past. The need for this could come, for example, as a result of logical errors, usually user errors, which lead to a loss of data. A system would then have to be set back to before these errors occurred. In the APO system environment, point-in-time recovery is a new element. We are no longer dealing with a point-in-time recovery for a single system, but rather for a system landscape, because consistency must guaranteed across the entire system landscape. From a purely technical point of view, this option seems viable, but there are application-related reasons that rule out the possibility of a point-in-time recovery. Let us assume, for example, that a planning run was carried out, and after this, a production order was sent. In the event of a point-in-time recovery, this production order would have to be recalled. A true point-in-time recovery is therefore not possible, so we will not discuss the technical possibilities.

7.4.2 Recovery to Completely Restore the Current Situation

Because of the architecture of APO systems, a crash can affect various components of the system. After recovering a component, you must also re-establish consistency with the other components. We can differentiate between the following cases:

▶ **The APO DB crashes**
In this case, you need to carry out a recovery with the resources of the RDBMS used. (The procedure is the same as for the SAP R/3 system, so we will assume that you are familiar with it.) You must then re-establish consistency between the APO DB, the liveCache, and the dedicated systems.

▶ **The liveCache crashes**
In this case, the APO DB is not affected, but the APO system as a whole either is unavailable, or has only limited availability. For this situation, recovery covers the liveCache.

▶ **The APO DB and the liveCache crash**

The recovery can be started in parallel. In this case, recovery means that old data backups can be run again in the APO DB and the live-Cache at the same time.

The following steps are involved in the recovery:

Preparations 1. Due to the fact that with each crash on the APO system, the dedicated R/3 or OLTP systems are also indirectly affected, it is recommended that your first step is to interrupt the transfer of data from these systems. You can get an overview of the dedicated systems that send data to the APO system using transaction **/SAPAPO/C2** of the APO system. If the APO system is no longer available, you will, of course, be unable to use this transaction. You will then need to know which systems are the dedicated systems, or you will need to check every one of the other possible systems for connections to the APO system. (To avoid this extra work, you should keep documentation or an administration manual that contains this information.) Log onto the dedicated systems. Stop the outbound queues going to the damaged APO system, using transaction **SMQ1** or the report program RSTRFCQ1. The queues will probably be stopped at some stage by an error message, if the APO system is no longer available. Before reaching this point, however, the source system will have made numerous attempts to send its requests. This will create extra load on the source system and should therefore be avoided.

2. Analyze the crash situation. If an APO DB recovery is necessary, the technical procedure to be followed is the same as for R/3 systems. Carry out the complete recovery using the appropriate RDBMS resources and/or SAPDBA. Then the APO system can once again be used for data transfer. However, if the liveCache is affected, certain characteristics must be taken into account. The APO instance remains available if the liveCache goes down, and as a result, user actions can lead to runtime errors. It is therefore recommended that you lock the APO system against other activities. These may include:

   ▶ **User activities**
   User activities can easily be stopped by locking all users in the APO system. For this you can use report program /SAPAPO/OM_LOCK-USER, which also supports the removal of the lock after the completion of the recovery. Please note that users already logged on to the system are not automatically logged off.

► **Background jobs**
Use transaction **SM36**, which you already know from R/3 systems, to reschedule background jobs that may be running during the recovery process.

► **Handling queues**
Here, we have to differentiate between operation with and without inbound queues. If you are using inbound queues and the APO instance is not affected by the crash, it is sufficient to stop processing of the inbound queue using transaction **SMQ2** or the report program RSTRFCI1. In principle, data transfer from the sending systems can be continued during the liveCache recovery. If, on the other hand, you have only outbound queues in your system landscape, the outbound queues in the dedicated systems must be halted.

In older versions of the APO system 3.0, there is, unfortunately, no special function for locking users in the APO system. In such a case, the following tp command, for example, can be used from operating system level.

tp locksys <SID>

With this command the APO system is locked against all users except for user DDIC. Attempts to logon are terminated with a message that says that an upgrade is currently active. This message does not actually mean what it says, but it achieves the desired objective of protecting the APO system from unwanted user activity. Once the recovery process is complete, the APO system can once again be released from the lock with the following command:

tp unlocksys <SID>

3. Recovery of the liveCache can be started only after all of this preparation work is complete. As you know from RDBMS, you start by restoring the last complete backup of the liveCache. This type of restore is carried out with DBMGUI, as described in Chapter 5.2.3. DBMGUI supports you in your selection of the backup by displaying the history of all backups carried out.

Recovery of the complete backup

4. After the restore is complete you can generally continue with the recovery of the log information. If the necessary log data is still in the log areas, the liveCache can be started. Data from the log is then automatically created again. However, if the log information has to be recreated by an external medium, the liveCache cannot be started. If an attempt to restart the liveCache is made, the liveCache will recognize

Recovery for liveCache 7.4

that its contents do not match the contents of the log, and will refuse the restart. For liveCache 7.4, in the next steps you have to recover the subsequent log backups or restore the incremental backups. The same rules apply as with normal RDBMS. Several media can be used in parallel for the restore and recovery. Here also we can assume that there will be a proportional improvement in performance if several media are used. We can say, as a rule of thumb, that restoring the data takes about the same time as creating the complete backup.

5. Once the necessary backups (data and log) have been recovered, the liveCache can be started. You should not use DBMGUI to do this, however. For the APO system to register the liveCache restart, you must start by using the relevant functions in transaction **LC10**.

6. Normal work can now resume in the APO system, meaning that the lock on users can be released and background jobs can run again. You should restart queues in stages, if possible, because there may by now be a high number of requests.

Recovery with liveCache 7.2

Since liveCache 7.2 does not have any physical logging, step 4 in the recovery scenario is different from that for liveCache 7.4. With release 7.2 you should under no circumstances use DBMGUI to transfer the liveCache to *warm* (*online*) mode. Recovery should first be resumed with the help of the APO system.

Logging with checkpoints

If you do not write a log in liveCache release 7.2 and only write checkpoints at discrete points in time, in the event of a recovery you will always experience some loss of data. In these circumstances, a roll forward of the liveCache is not possible. After restoring the backup, your next steps must be to restore consistency between the liveCache and the APO DB and between the APO system and the dedicated R/3 systems. The time it will take to recreate the liveCache and re-establish consistency between the data areas depends to a great extent on the data volume.

Alternatively, when logging with *checkpoint*, you can take into account the initialization of the entire liveCache with subsequent initial data transfer from the connected R/3 systems. In this way you can limit your losses to APO-specific data such as planning versions. You have to decide which method of procedure is most suitable in each case, based on the possible loss of data and the time needed for each procedure.

Recovery with synchronous logging

With synchronous logging, apart from the checkpoint, every change made between two checkpoints is recorded in the APO DB on object level. Recovery of the liveCache is therefore automatically resumed when the

`/SAPAPO/OM_LC_RECOVERY` program starts. First this report program stops the program scheduled to write the checkpoint, `/SAPAPO/OM_CHECKPOINT_WRITE`. Next, the recovery of the log from the APO DB is scheduled as a background job. You can decide whether or not any archive logs are to be included, as usual. When the recovery is complete, the liveCache is automatically restarted. Both inbound and outbound queues are also started again automatically. An e-mail is sent to the administrator to inform him or her of the completion of the process. The time taken to complete the procedure depends, first and foremost, on the volume of data to be restored. You can determine the size of the data volume in the logs using transaction **/SAPAPO/OM11**. The number of records in table */sapapo/lc_logh** is decisive. For each checkpoint and the associated log switch, the number in the column named **Number** is noted. As a rule of thumb you can estimate around 30 minutes for 100,000 to 150,000 records. You should also bear this in mind when setting the frequency of checkpoints.

You should start liveCache 7.2 only with APO resources; otherwise, it will not be possible to synchronize the APO system and the liveCache. If you start the liveCache using other tools (such as DBMGUI), it will be started in read-only mode. This situation is indicated by an amber traffic light symbol in the status display in transaction **LC10**.

After the completion of the recovery you must schedule report program `/SAPAPO/OM_ CHECKPOINT_WRITE` again.

Since no logging is available for the DP module in APO 3.0 with liveCache 7.2, this means that in the event of a crash there will always be a loss of data in this area. If you use DP, you must therefore continue with the recovery to deal with the DP data. There are different ways to do this:

DP data

▶ If a more recent backup of DP data is available in InfoCubes (see Chapter 7.5), the data can be reloaded from there. This is described in detail in APO documentation. Please note that this procedure may take a long time, at least as long as creating copies of DP data in InfoCubes.

▶ Inconsistencies between the APO DB and the liveCache can be detected using the report program `/SAPAPO/TS_CONS_CHECK_ALL`. To keep the recovery time for liveCache 7.2 to a minimum, this check can be limited to the active planning versions.

▶ If any inconsistencies are found between the APO DB and the liveCache, consistency can be restored using report program `/SAPAPO/TS_CONS_ CHECK`. Restoring consistency in this way usually means deleting the parts of the APO DB or the liveCache for which there are no counterparts in the other components of the APO DB or the liveCache.

Only after these steps have been completed can the APO system be released for all users, and queues and background processing can run once again.

If both the APO DB and the liveCache are affected by the crash, the recovery of the APO DB and the liveCache can be done at the same time. In this case, starting the liveCache in *warm* (*online*) mode should also be done with the help of the APO instance from transaction **LC10**. Only when the entire APO system is active once again can data transfer be resumed.

Recovery of an R/3 System

If an R/3 system is affected by a crash, your first step should also be to stop the outbound queue going from the APO system to the R/3 system. The recovery procedure itself is as normal.

7.4.3 Consequences

When an APO system is introduced into a system landscape, the recovery of an individual system becomes more complex. Particular attention should be paid to the links between the systems. Recovery no longer means simply retrieving backups in a database. You must also coordinate the stopping and restarting of data transfer between the systems and components. The situation is particularly critical if, due to a series of unfortunate circumstances, it is not possible to carry out a complete recovery of a system or an APO component. In this case you need to reestablish consistency in the system and components by comparing and adjusting imbalances (see Chapter 7 above). High-availability solutions gain relevance as a result.

In this respect, liveCache version 7.4 behaves similarly to other RDBMS. You can use the general failover solutions or run a shadow liveCache. For version 7.2, on the other hand, no real high-availability solution exists. In the event of a crash, you must always take manual measures such as /SAPAPO/OM_LC_RECOVERY or create consistency for DP data, to enable the liveCache to run on another machine.

An initialization of the liveCache should be avoided at all costs. This would be the same as starting planning activities in the APO system from scratch, which means that planning data accumulated up to now would be lost.

After initialization, all transaction data must be transferred from the dedicated R/3 system again. You can therefore see that the initialization of the liveCache is no substitute for a functional backup and recovery strategy.

7.5 Demand Planning: Backup into InfoCubes

If you begin the planning process in Demand Planning, demand forecasts are generated on the basis of historical data. As discussed in Chapter 1, data for the Demand Planning module is stored in InfoCubes, similarly to BW. When customizing, the application user decides which data is relevant to planning. Key figures relevant to planning are stored in the live-Cache to speed up the planning process. You can find information on which data are stored in the liveCache and which are stored in InfoCubes in the APO DB as follows:

1. Select **Demand Planning · Environment · Current Settings · Administration Demand Planning and Supply Network Planning** or call transaction **/SAPAPO/MSDP_ADMIN**. You will get an overview of all planning areas (see Figure 7.4).

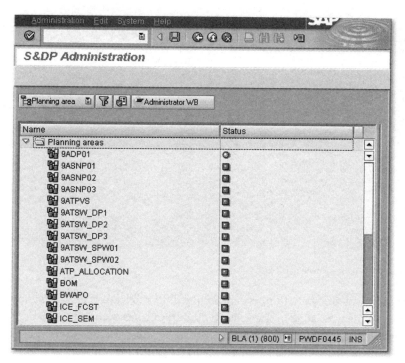

Figure 7.4 Overview of existing planning areas

2. Select the desired planning area with the mouse button on the right.

3. Select **Change.**

4. Confirm the ensuing security question.

5. Change to the **Key figures** area.

6. Change to the detailed display of key figures.

The entries in the column **InfoCube** show whether the key figures are stored in this InfoCube in the APO DB (see Figure 7.5). If there is no entry in the column, the key figures are maintained in the liveCache. If the key figures of an entire planning area are maintained in the liveCache, then in the APO DB there is a standardized InfoCube containing only the structure of the planning area and links to the key figures in the liveCache. For reasons of performance, key figures related to planning are normally stored in the liveCache.

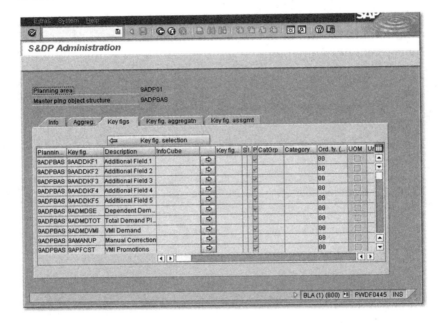

Figure 7.5 Planning areas and key figures

Backup into
InfoCubes
For purposes of evaluation, it can be useful to replicate the information stored in the liveCache in specially created InfoCubes in the APO DB or to transport them to a connected BW system. This procedure is referred to as a backup of Demand Planning data in (backup) InfoCubes. As already discussed in Chapter 1, where possible, BW tools and evaluations should not be used in the APO system, for reasons of performance. The structure

of the APO system is not optimized for BW evaluations. Such evaluations would even hinder the real planning activity in the APO system. It is therefore strongly advised that you transfer the necessary Demand Planning data via backups in InfoCubes to a BW system and evaluate the data there as you wish.

For liveCache version 7.2, such replication of Demand Planning in Info-Cubes is one way of saving Demand Planning data separately. This is of particular significance when we remember that liveCache 7.2 does not support logging for Demand Planning.

You can find a detailed description of how to carry out such a backup in APO documentation under *Extract data from a planning area*. The relevant departments usually decide which planning areas are suited to data extraction. Customizing the process is therefore also a task of the departments. The extraction is carried out in a background job, which can be absolutely critical to performance. This job should therefore be coordinated with other resource-intensive jobs—a task that falls within the scope of system administration. The procedure applies to every planning area. With liveCache 7.2 it is better to increase the frequency of checkpoints rather than the frequency of backups in InfoCubes.

Loading from InfoCubes

It is also possible to carry out the opposite procedure, that is, to load data from InfoCubes. Once again, you can find a description of how to do this in the APO documentation under *Loading to a planning area*. This procedure can be used to restore Demand Planning data in liveCache 7.2. Reloading data from InfoCubes is critical to performance, just as when writing to them. From a technical point of view, this is another reason why for liveCache 7.2 it is better to use more frequent checkpoints with synchronous backup of the liveCache than to make increased use of saving Demand Planning data to backup InfoCubes.

8 Consistency Checks

With the exchange of data between systems and the distribution of data over individual components, the question of data consistency arises.

When a system group is formed with the help of an APO system, the active exchange of data between the systems begins. Selected master and transaction data is sent from the dedicated systems to the APO system, and once there, it is distributed between the APO DB and the liveCache. Specific planning activities are carried out in the APO system; business objects created as a result of these activities are sent back to the dedicated systems.

Consistency means that the business objects are appropriate in terms of logical contexts and processes. It is difficult to check such consistency with technical resources because only certain data can be compared in this way. In view of these constraints, SAP AG offers what are known as *consistency checks*, although the name *data comparator* might be more accurate. The consistency checks can never compare faulty interfaces or operating defects; they can only be used to check business objects up to a certain level of detail. In principle, the CIF (Core Interface) and the system architecture of the APO system guarantee the consistency of data. Nevertheless, inconsistencies can occur, particularly in the following cases:

Data comparison

▶ If it has been necessary to carry out a complete recovery in one of the systems in the system group, the APO DB, or the liveCache.

▶ If a point-in-time recovery has been carried out in a system, the APO DB, or the liveCache.

▶ If objects in the queues are deleted during data exchange.

▶ If there are software errors.

In these cases the consistency checks can be extremely helpful. You should bear in mind, however, that only certain elements of the business objects can be checked. In the worst cases, not all inconsistencies are found and resolved accordingly. In general, when speaking of consistency we can differentiate between what are termed *external* and *internal consistency*.

8.1 Internal Consistency

The APO system operates with two data retention systems: the APO DB and the liveCache. By *internal consistency* we refer to the consistency of the data in these two components (see Figure 8.1). The distribution of data between the APO DB and the liveCache was discussed in Chapter 1. In order for the APO system to run accurately, the data fragments in the APO DB and in the liveCache must be consistent after a transaction has been completed. During a transaction, temporary inconsistencies may occur, but on completion of the transaction, these are corrected in the course of the *commit*.

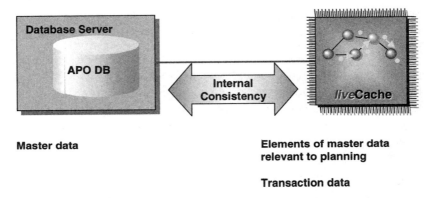

Figure 8.1 APO internal consistency between the APO DB and the liveCache

One way to check internal consistency is to use transaction **/SAPAPO/ OM17**. In order for the report program to run properly, all other system activities, including CIF transfer and background jobs, should be stopped. This will aid you in, for example, preventing temporary inconsistencies in uncompleted transactions from showing up as errors. In the initial screen of transaction **/SAPAPO/OM17**, the following functions are offered:

▶ Lock users

▶ Deallocate background jobs

▶ Stop the processing of inbound queues, if inbound queues are used

Figure 8.2 shows this initial screen.

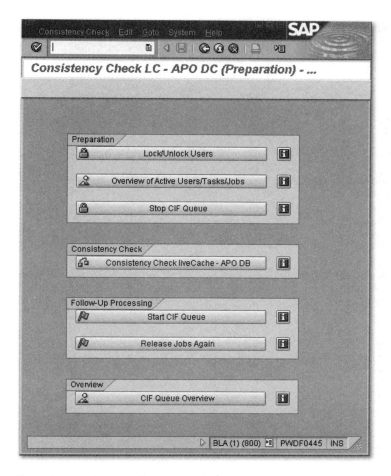

Figure 8.2 Initial screen of transaction /SAPAPO/OM17

With an APO system running around the clock, it would be very difficult to stop all system activities for consistency checks. Under these circumstances temporary inconsistencies could also mistakenly be identified as problematic inconsistencies. Because of this, the consistency check should be run twice and the intersection—that is to say, the shared average of the results—should be worked out.

The internal consistency check can be limited to selected business objects and related processes (see Figure 8.3). To do this, select function **Consistency Check liveCache – APO DB**.

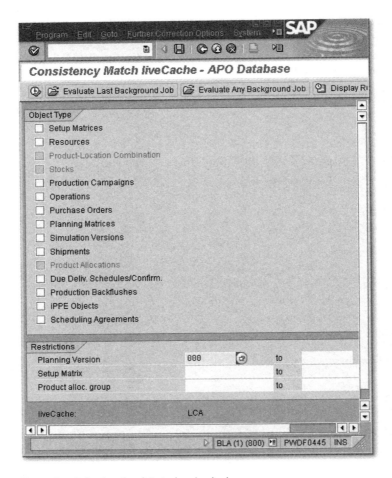

Figure 8.3 Selecting the data to be checked

Runtime The consistency check's runtime depends on the type and number of the objects selected. It is therefore not possible to offer any guidelines on how long the consistency check might take. Data comparison can be run in dialog mode or in the background. Due to the runtime, however, it is advisable to run it in the background. You can find information about the duration of data comparisons already run in the background by using the function **Consistency Check liveCache – APO DB · Display runtimes**.

Results log The results log of the checks carried out in dialog mode can be found via **Consistency Check liveCache – APO DB · Further correction options · Any online activities**. For consistency checks run in the background, use **Consistency Check liveCache – APO DB · Evaluate any background job**.

You can now start to correct the data. Corrections should always be based on the last up-to-date consistency check. You can find the corresponding log using **Evaluate last background job**, or if it is the result of an online comparison, it is displayed immediately. The options for making corrections depend largely on the type of object in question; parts of objects are contained in either the APO DB or the liveCache, but other objects or parts of objects may be held redundantly. Consistency is achieved by either deleting all the data in the APO DB that is not in the liveCache, or vice versa. Only parts held redundantly can be reconstructed. In addition to the correction possibilities offered by transaction **/SAPAPO/OM17**, objects can be corrected manually using application resources. If you use only the resources of transaction **/SAPAPO/OM17**, then after the transaction has been completed, the data contained in the APO DB and the liveCache will be the data that was available in both. In mathematical terms, this means the common intersection. The result of this, however, is that data is usually lost, which can be re-compiled by the application only by manually repeating the appropriate transactions.

Correction

In APO 3.0, the consistency check has only limited functions. You will find further details on this in SAPNet Note 425825.

APO 3.0

From these observations, we can see that checking the consistency of data is not a purely technical task. The technical systems administrator can indeed run transaction **/SAPAPO/OM17**, but to evaluate the results or even to remedy the inconsistencies you need application know-how— that is to say, you must be familiar with the application. You therefore need to ensure that there are clear communication structures and clearly defined areas of responsibility between the areas of basic technical expertise and application expertise in your enterprise.

Technical and application know-how

To keep the runtime of internal consistency checks to a minimum, it may be acceptable to execute only the check for active planning versions. Inconsistencies in non-active planning versions—that is, versions not currently needed—do not interfere with current planning.

8.2 External Consistency

By external consistency we refer to the consistency of the dataset of an APO system in comparison to a dedicated system, such as an R/3 system (see Figure 8.4).

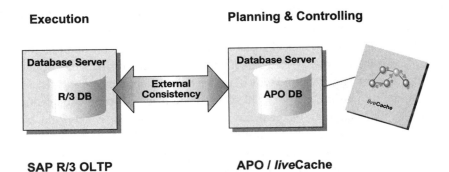

Execution **Planning & Controlling**

Database Server

R/3 DB

External Consistency

Database Server

APO DB

liveCache

SAP R/3 OLTP **APO / *live*Cache**

Figure 8.4 External consistency between a dedicated system and the APO system

As with internal consistency, there are limitations on automatically deter-mining or reestablishing the external consistency between the APO sys-tem and the dedicated systems. Here too, only the data offered and selected in the initial screen can be compared. The consistency check pro-vided by SAP can compare only data in an R/3 system with that in an APO system. External consistency checks can by no means replace the correct administration and monitoring of CIF data transfers. In order to obtain realistic results when checking external consistency, you must first confirm the internal consistency of the APO system. In addition, it is necessary that in both the APO system and the R/3 system to be compared, all other activities, including the processing of queues, are halted. If more than one R/3 system is linked to the APO system, any processing tasks for these other systems in the APO system queues must also be stopped. Only if all of these conditions are present can you assume that the results of the external consistency check will be accurate. If other system activities can-not be stopped, the external consistency check should also be run twice, or more often if necessary, to filter out temporary inconsistencies. Objects in the inbound or outbound queues are not included in the consistency check.

Figure 8.5 shows the selection screen for comparing external consistency. Since the APO dataset can be compared to only one dedicated system, you must first select the partner system and material, value, and integra-tion model, as required.

The data comparison for checking external consistency is executed by report program /SAPAPO/CIF_DELTAREPORT3. In addition to schedul-ing the report for background processing, you can also start it using trans-action **/SAPAPO/CCR** or, if you are beginning from transaction **/SAPAPO/**

OM17, you can start it via **Consistency Check liveCache – APO DB · Further Correction Options · CIF Compare/Reconcile Function**.

In older APO 3.0 systems, only the report program /SAPAPO/CIF_ DELTAREPORT, with limited functions, was available. For further details on the range of functions, see SAPNet Note 425825.

APO 3.0

For most objects you can only check whether the object exists; you cannot check its identity. If requests are found in the dedicated R/3 system that are not in the APO system, they can be transferred to the APO system and vice versa.

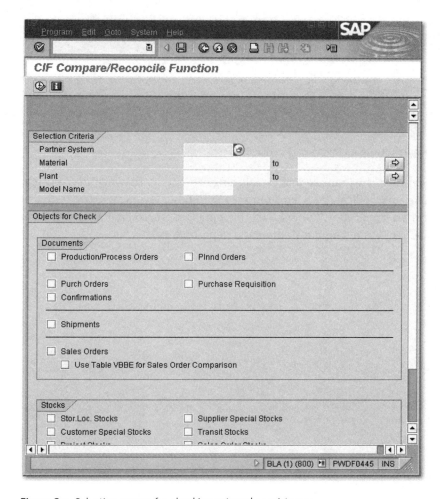

Figure 8.5 Selection screen for checking external consistency

Differences in delivery dates, for example, are not yet revealed. Figure 8.6 shows an example of a possible error log generated by the report program /SAPAPO/CIF_DELTAREPORT3.

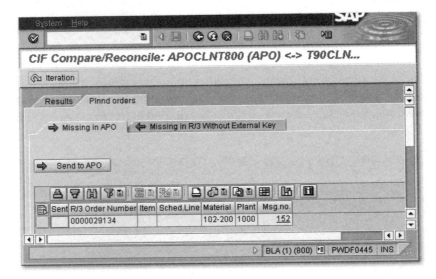

Figure 8.6 Result log of the external data comparison

Here again we can see that establishing consistency between the APO system and dedicated systems requires both basic technical knowledge and expert application know-how. This entails close collaboration between basic or system administration and departments.

9   Optimizers

The role of optimizers in the APO system is described in this chapter. Particular attention is paid to the administrative tasks for managing these components.

Optimizers can be included as components of an APO system alongside the APO DB and the liveCache. However, they are not absolutely necessary. Which and how many optimizers are implemented in an APO system depends on how the APO system is used. If optimizers should fail, only those functions of the APO system that use the optimizers are affected, and a problem with optimizers does not affect the overall availability of the system. Similarly, if other components in the APO system fail, this does not affect the optimizers.

Broadly speaking, the optimizers in an APO system are numeric programs based on mathematical algorithms that optimize interrelationships. Therefore, the applications provide them with input values, then they calculate an optimum and report this result back to the application. This simplified procedure demonstrates the main activity of optimizers: calculation. Unlike the APO DB and the liveCache, optimizers do not manage any data. Therefore, backups and recovery do not apply. You only need to carry out backups of the operating system and its file system from time to time.

Optimizers are actually optimization algorithms. The algorithms implemented in C++ are available as separate programs. SAP currently offers APO optimizers for the following areas:

Available optimizers

▶ Supply Network Planning (SNP)

▶ Production Planning and Detailed Scheduling (PP/DS)

▶ Vehicle Scheduling and Routing (VS)

▶ Order sequence optimizer (Sequencing)

▶ Capable-to-Match (CTM)

▶ Model mix (since APO 3.1)

It is also possible to add your own optimizers to the APO software, provided that they use the existing interfaces. Adding your own optimizers can make sense for customer-specific offcut optimizers, for example, as used in the timber and paper industries. From a technical point of view, these interfaces are BAPIs that can be used to exchange data. See APO documentation for a description of the BAPIs available.

Availability The APO optimizers are available only for Windows platforms; porting for other operating systems is not currently planned. The optimizers supplied by SAP are completely integrated into program flows. If an optimization program is called from within a transaction, the user can follow the progress of the optimization calculations on screen. To do this, the optimizers supplied by SAP use OCX to transmit data to the front-end, the SAP GUI.

Network The input values to be optimized are read from the work processes in the liveCache and the APO DB and transferred to the optimizer using RFCs. Only the PP/DS optimizer can access the liveCache directly. For this reason, when using the PP/DS optimizer, a high-performance network must be used between the liveCache and the PP/DS optimizer. For all other optimizers, an acceptably powerful network between the APO instance and the optimizer is sufficient. Figure 9.1 shows the interaction between optimizers, the APO instance, and the liveCache.

Discrete and continuous models In optimization, we can differentiate between discrete models and continuous models. *Discrete models* are used for planning products that can be produced only in whole-numbered units, such as cars. Lot sizes or minimum sizes can also be defined. *Continuous models* are used in the production of non-unit-based products like liquids.

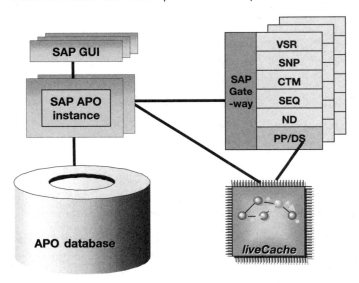

Figure 9.1 The correlation of APO components

For most optimizers, performance is dependent first and foremost on the calculation capacity of the processors. Around 512 Mb per optimizer should be sufficient. The SNP optimizer is an exception to this, because it works with complex models and therefore usually needs around 1 Gb. If you run several optimizers and need to use them in parallel, you will need access to the corresponding number of CPUs and sufficient memory. The limitations on memory associated with the Windows 32-bit operating system also apply to optimizers. It is not advisable to use optimizers on the same machine as the APO DB or the liveCache. Hardware requirements

You have to allow one CPU for each optimization process. (Again, the PP/DS optimizer is an exception to this rule.) With the appropriate customizing of the application, several CPUs can be used; you will need to discuss this with the application team. The high CPU load caused by optimizers means that they can quickly deprive the liveCache or the APO DB of the processing performance they need. Also, memory bottlenecks in the liveCache or the APO DB are critical, negatively impacting the entire APO system as well as slowing up the individual optimization step.

We recommend that before the start of the production operation, you simulate the optimization steps for planning, using the most realistic data possible. The time taken for optimization can vary considerably from case to case. It will depend on the number of iterations necessary for optimization, so you will not get a satisfactory forecast of how long it will take if you run only one test with only one set of values. You should do several optimization test runs, using different input values.

9.1 Installation

During installation of the APO system and its optimizers, one RFC connection, of type TCP/IP, is created for each optimizer server. During the creation of the RFC connection, the actual optimization program is allocated. You can check the settings using transaction **SM59** (see Figure 9.2). In this example the optimization program for PP/DS, *d:\apoopt\dps\bin\dsoptsvr.exe,* has been allocated.

Communication with the optimization program on the optimizer server is done via a gateway, with which you are familiar from R/3 instances; you can access the optimizer only if this gateway has been started. This gateway is also created during the installation of the optimizer, and is run as a Windows service. You can check the gateway settings by clicking on the **Gateway** button. The optimization processes are active only if they have been called. Gateway

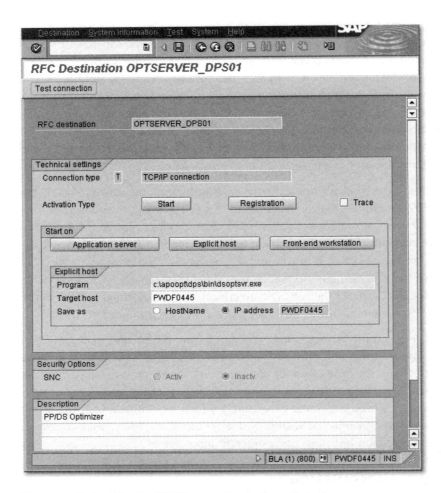

Figure 9.2 Customizing the TCP/IP connection to the optimization program

The PP/DS optimizer should be installed and operated on every optimizer server regardless of whether it is to be used for planning or not, since it supports certain management tasks for all other optimizers. For example, you can use transaction **/SAPAPO/OPT09** to display the version of the individual optimization programs. This function is provided only by the PP/DS optimizer. The PP/DS optimizer can also be used to display all processes on the optimizer server. You can use transaction **/SAPAPO/OPT12** to do this.

All settings for optimizers can be made using the SAP Reference IMG. To do this, start transaction **SPRO · SAP Reference IMG · APO Implementation Guide · Advanced Planner and Optimizer · Base Settings · Optimi-**

zation · **Basic functions**. You can customize the installed optimizers via the menu **Maintain global settings** or by using transaction **/SAPAPO/COPT01** (see Figure 9.3).

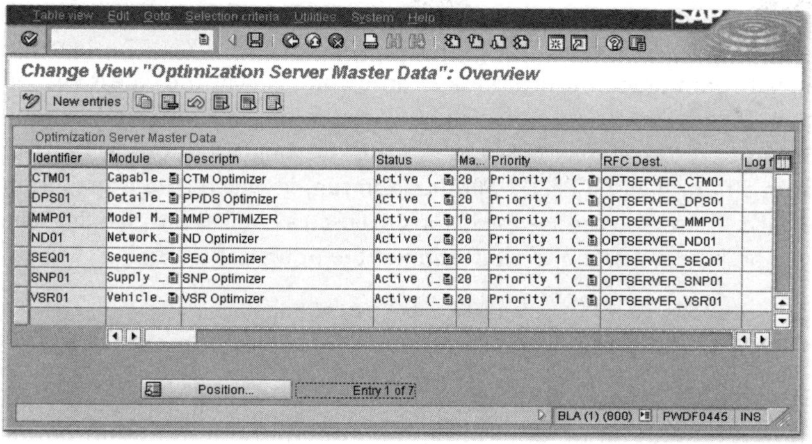

Figure 9.3 Customizing optimizers

You can control how optimizers are used, especially if several optimizers are installed. For instance, you can define a maximum number of users. Once this limit has been reached, no other users will be given access to this optimizer. Additional users are automatically diverted to other similar optimizers, if they are available.

You can set a priority so that users are diverted to optimizers preferentially. In the column **Log file**, a directory can be allocated to the CTM optimizer for the log files that will be written. The name of the file will be given automatically by the system. For all other optimizers, the log file is always written to the working directory in the gateway.

Thus far, the logging level is not yet influenced by the selection in the **Status** column in the display of transaction **/SAPAPO/COPT01**. The content of the log can be displayed from those applications that use the optimizer. You can also find the optimization log of the SNP optimizer, for example, using the menu steps **Supply Network Planning · Evaluations · Optimizer log data.** The optimization log can also be displayed independently of the application using transaction **/SAPAPO/OPT11**. Here you will find a history of the last optimization runs and the corresponding logs; each optimization run and the individual optimization steps are logged. You can analyze the trace file for the optimization run using **Additions · Display trace file**. It is true that trace files are rather technical in nature and usually very long, but they do contain essential details on the optimization run. For the PP/DS optimizer, for example, you can see precisely when the live-Cache was accessed.

In the first part of the optimization run, data is read from the liveCache using the COM routine SAPAPO_OPT_GET_ACTIVITY_NET. Then the actual optimization calculations are carried out. Finally, the data is written back to the liveCache. This is done with the help of the COM routine SAPAPO_OPT_ UPDATE_ACTIVITY_NET. Listing 9.1 shows an extract from a trace file of a PP/DS optimization run, in which data is read from the liveCache. You can see the logon data used as well as the planning version and the transactional simulation of the optimization run.

```
for reading... []connecting to liveCache...
<2> 19:56:28 live_connection_ntintel.cpp(740) 'Module_
LC' Entering connection function
<2> 19:56:28 live_connection_ntintel.cpp(741) 'Module_
LC' serverDB:          LCA
<2> 19:56:28 live_connection_ntintel.cpp(742) 'Module_
LC' serverLocation:    us04d1
<2> 19:56:28 live_connection_ntintel.cpp(743) 'Module_
LC' userName:          SAPR3
<2> 19:56:28 live_connection_ntintel.cpp(744) 'Module_
LC' passwd ( ok!)
<i> 19:56:28 lcmodel_module.cpp(924) 'Module_
LC' connection to liveCache established.
<i> 19:56:28 lcmodel_module.cpp(928) 'Module_
LC' transferring data from liveCache...
<2> 19:56:28 live_connection_ntintel.cpp(780) 'Module_
LC' Entering getDataFromLC function:
<2> 19:56:28 live_connection_ntintel.cpp(781) 'Module_
LC' startTime: 1015801200
<2> 19:56:28 live_connection_ntintel.cpp(782) 'Module_
LC' endTime:   1018389600
<2> 19:56:28 live_connection_ntintel.cpp(783) 'Module_
LC' VersionID: "4Gr0RX3MBa2hyZpi14Gq1W"
<2> 19:56:28 live_connection_ntintel.cpp(784) 'Module_
LC' Planning_versionID: "000"
<2> 19:56:28 live_connection_ntintel.cpp(785) 'Module_
LC' Client: 001
<2> 19:56:28 live_connection_ntintel.cpp(890) 'Module_
LC' Now Calling COM-Object SAPAPO_OPT_GET_ACTIVITY_NET:
```

```
. . .
<i> 19:56:28 lcmodel_module.cpp(973) 'Module_
LC' ...end of transfer.
<i> 19:56:28 lcmodel_module.cpp(979) 'Module_
LC' disconnecting from liveCache...
```
Listing 9.1 Extract from a trace file of a PP/DS optimization run

Please note that when executing the report program /SAPAPO/OM_
LCCHECK, optimizers are also addressed in a test mode. The background
job discussed in the previous chapter, based on the report program
/SAPAPO/OM_REORG_DAILY cleans out obsolete optimization logs. You
can use transaction **/SAPAPO/COPT00** to define how long the log files
should be kept. The option **Log expiration in days** determines how long
the log files will be kept.

You can also define a failover solution using transaction
/SAPAPO/COPT00. If several optimizers are available, one can be given
priority 9—the lowest priority level (transaction **/SAPAPO/COPT01**). If
you set the flag **Check server availability,** the availability of the optimization server is checked before the optimizer is started, using the `ping` command. In this way, you can quickly detect when an optimizer fails and
there is an automatic switch to another optimizer. You can, of course, get
a similar function with commercial failover solutions such as MSCS
(*Microsoft Cluster Service*). Before implementing comprehensive high-
availability solutions for optimizers, however, you should discuss with the
relevant departments how important the optimizers are for the overall
functioning of the APO system group.

Reliability

You can also use several optimization processes for optimizing PP/DS
planning, using transaction **/SAPAPO/COPT02**. In Customizing, you can
define how many optimization processes (agents), working on different
aspects, can search for an optimal solution at the same time. A solution
will not necessarily be found more quickly via this method, but a better
solution will likely be found. If, during an optimization run, it is established that one optimization approach moves a process away from the
optimum, this process can be terminated by the user or the optimizer. The
optimization process that is now free can automatically be allocated a new
subtask. If you were to represent this optimization technique in a simple
model, you could divide the optimization problem up into several subtrees. Each process could work on one subtree. From the results, the user
could choose what he or she considers to be the optimal solution.

Multi-agent optimization for PP/DS

The application forms the backdrop for multi-agent optimization, but the consequences are technical. To date, multi-agent optimization for PP/DS is not accommodated in the Quick Sizer; if you are going to use the method described above, the optimizer server should have as many CPUs as are used in the customizing process. From a technical point of view, the number of processes specified, plus an extra process for optimization, are used. The additional process is used only for communication between the actual optimization processes.

9.2 Monitoring

The architecture and functions of optimizers have a simple structure, so only a few monitoring tasks are necessary. Usage of optimization processes is closely linked with planning activities in the APO system. Optimizers are not used regularly, nor are they used with a constant load. Rather, they are needed at certain times during certain planning steps. For this reason, monitoring is needed mainly while optimizers are being used. This is another example of the importance of communication between system administrators and the various departments; in order to guarantee a stable operation of the APO system, the system administrators must have as precise a picture as possible of the processes in the APO system. The following aspects should be taken into account when monitoring an optimization server:

▶ **The number of users during an optimization run**
You can use transaction **/SAPAPO/OPT03** to get an overview of all users currently working with optimizers.

▶ **Bottlenecks in hardware use**
For this, you can use the operating system monitor **OS06**. You will find more detailed instructions for installation in Chapter 11. The rules for evaluating the operating system statistics, which we assume you know from R/3 systems, can for the most part be transferred to the optimization server (see also [Schneider 2001]).

▶ **An overview of all processes on the optimization server**
You can use the menu function **Tools · APO administration · Optimization · System monitoring · Process** overview, or transaction **/SAPAPO/OPT12,** to ensure that other activities on the optimization server do not lead to bottlenecks. This function is provided by the PP/DS optimizer and is therefore available only when this optimizer is active on the server.

Should errors occur during the optimization run, you are advised to use logging. In this case, the familiar SAP system tools, such as the system log, application log, runtime error overview, and COM trace, and the Windows Event Log on the optimization server, can also offer useful information about possible problems.

10 Authorizations

In this chapter we will examine the new authorizations asso-
ciated with APO systems and discuss their most important dif-
ferences with regard to R/3 systems. We will pay particular
attention to the roles that affect the system administrator.

10.1 General Considerations

The APO authorization concept follows the same authorization concept
with which you are familiar from R/3 systems. Therefore, tools such as the
profile generator or the granting of authorization can be used in the same
way in APO systems. The difference between R/3 and APO systems lies in
the objects they contain.

Special user roles have been predefined for working with the APO system.
Each role combines a number of authorizations, and fulfills the typical
field of activity of an APO user. Several roles can be combined to create a
new role as required. Figure 10.1 shows the roles that can generally be
assigned in an APO system, if all functions are used.

You can display all of the known authorization objects in the APO system
using transaction **SU21**. The APO-specific authorization objects in the
application are grouped together in the APO object class.

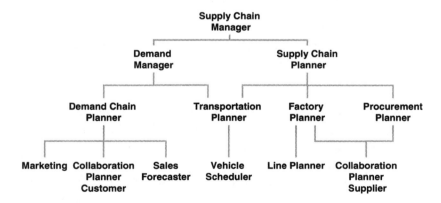

Figure 10.1 The structure of roles

10.2 Authorizations for liveCache Administration

Authorization objects associated with liveCache administration belong to the object class BC-A. For APO 3.1, since Basis Support Package 16 there have been four roles available for liveCache system administration:

▶ SAP_BC_LVC_USER
This role is only for monitoring the functional efficiency of the live-Cache. All of the display functions in transaction **LC10** can be used. Changes of any kind to liveCache configuration and integration are stopped.

▶ SAP_BC_LVC_OPERATOR
In addition to monitoring, this authorization allows the user to start and stop the liveCache. No changes can be implemented.

▶ SAP_BC_LVC_ADMINISTRATOR
In addition to monitoring, starting, and stopping, this role also allows changes to the configuration, parameters, and integration data of the liveCache. Administrators can also define and change additional connections to external liveCaches. However, initialization of a liveCache is not possible.

▶ SAP_BC_LVC_SUPERUSER
The super user is allowed to carry out all tasks related to the liveCache. Most notably, the super user can initialize a liveCache. This role should be assigned very restrictively. The initialization of a liveCache is to be avoided at all costs, even in a development system.

Please note that liveCache system administration is also included in R/3 software, thanks to transaction **LC10**. If you are operating an R/3 4.6D and are managing liveCaches belonging to APO systems from here, you can use the roles for liveCache administration as they are used in APO systems.

APO 3.0

These user roles are not available in APO 3.0. Authorizations to live-Cache administration must be compiled manually. Many displays of statistics in the liveCache are based on the execution of external operating system commands. As a result, it is absolutely necessary that the liveCache system administrator have the authorization *S_LOG_COM*. Otherwise, the liveCache status display will fail, and this could easily be taken to mean that the liveCache is inactive.

10.3 Data Exchange

Certain important authorizations are necessary for the exchange of data between the APO and R/3 systems in addition to the authorizations and roles of users in the APO system. To date, SAP does not supply any pre-defined profiles and roles for users in the R/3 and APO systems that should be used when data is being exchanged between two systems. There must be a user in both the R/3 system and the APO system. All incoming or outgoing CIF requests are allocated to this user and processed. The necessary authorizations depend mainly on the objects to be exchanged between the systems and how they are to be processed, which in turn depends on the application modules used. As this is very customer-specific, it is up to the customer to define the necessary user authorization profile for exchanging data on the R/3 and the APO sides.

The following considerations should be taken into account:

▶ The user who will exchange the data must have the same name in the APO system as in the R/3 system. This user ID should be used only for data transfer, since this facilitates error analysis.

▶ The user should not be a *dialog* user. You should use the *service* user-type, so that this user ID cannot be used in dialog mode. If you are using ATP, a *service* user can be used only with APO 3.0. Please note that with the *service* user-type, it is not possible to carry out debugging or to replace values during debugging. If debugging is required in a test system or quality assurance system, you must define a *dialog* user for the data exchange.

▶ For data transfer from an R/3 system to the APO system, a user with the authorization *S_RFC* is required in the APO system.

▶ When transferring data from the APO system to the R/3 system, the user in the R/3 system must have all authorizations to be able to process the transferred data. A very vague statement, admittedly, but it is difficult to give a more precise general statement, since the necessary authorizations are largely dependent on the specific case. Nevertheless, we recommend that you try to avoid the simplest solution, which would be to give the user the authorization *SAP_ALL*. To do so would mean that all doors in your R/3 system would be wide open for any user who can use RFC functions in the APO system. In any case, the authorization concept *S_ TCODE* should be withdrawn for the R/3 user when exchanging data. The authorization *SAP_ALL* contains this authorization object with the value *, which means that the execution of all transactions is permitted. This could even include, for example, the creation of a new user. You should therefore remove this right from users who are exchanging data. Furthermore, the user should not hold the authorization object *S_DEVELOP*. Authorizations based on object this allow changes to be made to data in the ABAP Dictionary, or can be used for ABAP programming.

Currently, the only method for reducing CIF users' authorizations to the necessary and sufficient is to record all authorizations with a trace that is activated only for authorization objects. To do so, call transaction **ST01**. Activate the trace only for CIF users and only for authorizations. One problem with this method is that the trace usually has to remain active over a long period of time. You must ensure that all relevant actions are executed during this timeframe. You should also bear in mind that in a production system, a representative period can last up to a month. During this period, usage of the APO system changes, and with it the objects transferred to the R/3 system. APO users start DP, start planning runs for data transfer to SNP, execute SNP planning, start the SNP heuristic run or the optimizing run for data transfer to the PP/DS, and so on. You need a representative authorization trace for all of these planning steps. For reasons of security, you should not avoid this task. You should also use a meaningful test of procedures before the start of production operation.

11 Performance Monitoring and Tuning

This chapter describes the most important tools for evaluating the performance of an APO system. Statistics that you know from R/3 systems are interpreted differently in APO systems.

The performance of a system is always perceived as the concrete response time when a user executes operations on the SAP GUI. Compared to R/3, the APO system has more components and more cross-system functions. As a result, it is decidedly more difficult for the system administrator to locate a bottleneck. Figure 11.1 shows the interaction of numerous components in an APO system. Due to a combination of different circumstances or unfortunate situations, each component can contribute to a general loss of performance.

11.1 Preparation

Some analysis tools must be installed to enable you to assess the performance of an APO system.

11.1.1 Operating System Monitor

As you know from R/3 systems, you can use the program `saposcol` to collect statistics on the use of hardware in the individual application servers. Transaction **OS07** prepares this data and allows you to estimate whether there are or have been resource bottlenecks on the servers, and if so, to pinpoint what they are. For servers in a system group that do not have any R/3-like instances, such as optimization servers or a separate liveCache server, the collection of operating system statistics has to be configured explicitly.

One possibility is to install the program `rfcoscol`, as described in SAP-Net Notes 20624 and 202934.

rfcoscol

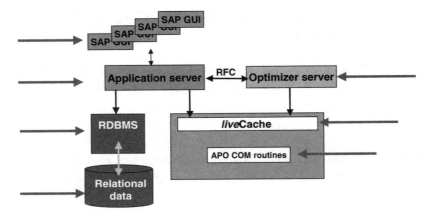

Figure 11.1 APO components that influence performance

From R/3 Basis release 4.6B on, it is possible to use CCMS agents to collect data. To do this, the operating system collector `saposcol` is installed on the server to be monitored. a *CCMS agent* is also installed on the server to forward the data to a selected central system. All statistics related to the use of resources on the remote servers are thus available on this central server. This central system can be the APO instance, or any other SAP system. It is important that this SAP system runs Basis release 4.6B, at least. You will find a detailed description of the installation procedure in SAPNet Notes 371023 and 450741.

If you use this technique, you can select one system as the central monitoring system of your system group. The CCMS alert monitor, transaction **RZ20**, forms the core of central monitoring. We will assume that you are familiar with the functions of the alert monitor from R/3 systems. With the introduction of APO systems and the closer connection between systems that comes with it, the alert monitor gains even more importance as the central monitoring node in the system landscape.

11.1.2 CCMS Alert Monitor RZ20

Important indicators for liveCache operation are included in the software from Basis release 4.6D on. You can activate them using transaction **LC10**. (However, the APO 3.0 system is based on release 4.6C.) In order to monitor several liveCaches centrally with the help of the alert monitor **RZ20**, we recommend the following solution:

Many administrative functions for the liveCache are included in SAP Basis software. As a result, from any R/3 system you can manage and, in particular, analyze liveCaches that do not belong to the same system. The only prerequisite is that the R/3 system must have Basis release 4.6D or higher. In transaction **LC10** a connection must be made for each liveCache to be monitored. In Chapter 3 we have already described how the alert monitor can be activated for qRFC in old R/3 and APO systems. Figure 11.2 shows how central monitoring can be set up.

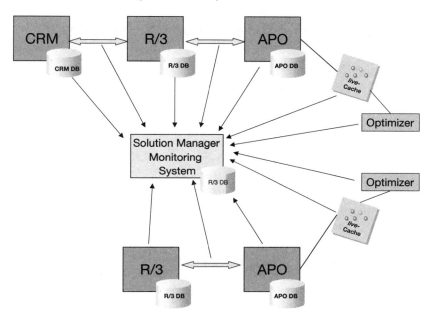

Figure 11.2 Central monitoring with the Solution Manager

By combining these aspects, you can use the alert monitor to set up central monitoring for the system landscape. We recommend that you use the following procedure to do so:

1. For central monitoring, select an especially stable SAP system. Stability is essential because monitoring is needed at all times. This system should not be a production system, because this would bring with it the disadvantage that you would have to worry about data security. Also, in the worst case, the monitoring load can have a negative effect on production operation, even if the load is relatively low. In a production system, Basis Support Packages needed for monitoring would also have to be checked more closely for compatibility. Taking all of these aspects into account, it becomes clear that the central monitoring system is best run on an additional R/3 system that is specially installed for this purpose. It would also be sufficient to run what is known as a *mini*

SAP Basis system. A mini SAP Basis system is an SAP demo system that contains only Basis software components and objects. You can order it from the SAP Web site.

2. Configure the alert monitor **RZ20** for the systems in the system landscape to be monitored and for their components. The operating system monitor can be activated for servers even if they are on non-SAP systems. The alert monitor also supports, for example, sending e-mails in the event of errors or when user-definable threshold values are exceeded.

3. The third step is to install the Solution Manager in this special system. Since early 2002, the Solution Manager has been SAP AG's central support platform. Services offered by SAP, such as EarlyWatch or GoingLive, are executed in your system landscape with the help of the Solution Manager. SAP also offers *self services*, which each customer can order and execute independently. Furthermore, the Solution Manager works in collaboration with the alert monitor **RZ20**. In this way, the Solution Manager makes it possible for you to use *central system administration* or *service level reporting*. You can also find details on this on the Internet in the SAP Service Marketplace.

11.2 Workload Analysis ST03N

You can use transaction **ST03N** to get an idea of how response times are distributed over the various components of the APO system. The older transaction for workload analysis, **ST03**, is not as useful in APO systems because the liveCache's response time cannot be displayed separately. Instead, the liveCache's response time is included in the processing time so that you can only speculate as to its actual share. For this reason, you should use the revised transaction **ST03N** for workload analysis in APO systems. This transaction supports different modes for users with different levels of expertise and different requirements. You can click a button to change between the modes *expert*, *administrator*, and *service engineer*. The descriptions below are based on administrator mode, in which all of the functions of transaction **ST03N** are available. Figure 11.3 shows an overview of the system load from administrator mode. Depending on the mode selected, certain functions on the left-hand side of the menu tree are hidden.

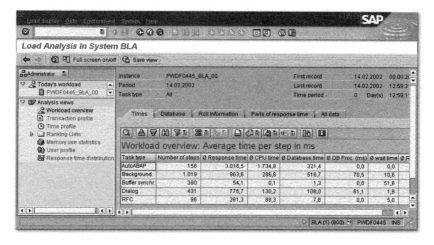

Figure 11.3 Workload overview

Similar to transaction **ST03**, the workload overview displays the different task types' shares in the overall response time. A new addition is the *DB proc.* time. This covers the time needed to send the request to the live-Cache and the time from the execution and processing of a COM routine until the results are transferred. The time needed for network transfer is thus included in DB proc. time. Should communication problems occur between the liveCache and the APO instances, this is reflected in very high times for the COM routines.

This type of network problem is best eliminated using the operating system function provided by SAP, known as *niping*. Use transaction **/SAPAPO/OM13 · Network** (see Chapter 6) to check the network connection. Using the `niping` command, you can measure the volume and the rate of transfer between the liveCache and the APO instance. The value calculated, `bw2`, should be as close as possible to the bandwidth used between the APO instance and the liveCache. As mentioned previously, a network with a bandwidth of at least 100 Mbits should be used between APO instances and the liveCache.

Communication problems

For R/3 systems, certain basic rules apply to the ratios of the individual times in the overall response time. For example, CPU time and DB time can each take up a maximum of 40% of the total response time. These rules can be applied directly to an APO system, but to date, there are no general rules for ideal ratios in response times. The reason for this lies in the very different possible uses of an APO system. Depending on usage, the time taken (by COM routines, in particular) can vary greatly. As we have explained above, it is also impossible to formulate general rules for the runtimes of individual COM routines. We can only recommend that by regularly monitoring your own APO system, you develop a feel for the "normal" ratios in response times for that particular system. If you should notice a marked, temporary change in response times, then you can anticipate a performance problem in the system.

You can find details on performance analysis in SAP systems in [Schneider 2002].

Testing the COM routines

One simple way to check the general response time for COM routines is to use the report program /SAPAPO/OM_PERFORMANCE. Select the default assignment in the initial screen and start the report, which will then generate the test data. Next, the COM routines are used to execute simple calculations. The runtime for these calculations with COM routines is measured for each task. With the default assignment of parameters, each calculation block should take around five seconds. These times may be considerably higher, especially if there are network problems. In any case, this procedure produces only a first approximation. The default assignment of parameters in this report as delivered by SAP are based solely on experience, obtained from concrete machines and installations at SAP. They are by no means binding.

Response time of the optimizers

Another feature particular to APO is the response times of optimizers. Until now, the response times of optimizers has been included in the RFC time in the statistics. The runtimes of the optimization steps can be determined only using the optimization log from transaction **/SAPAPO/OPT11**.

As is standard, for each transaction run in the system a statistics record is written with the corresponding response time ratios. However, by default, a separate proportionate statistics record is not written for the COM routines contained in the transaction. Writing this record must be activated explicitly. To do so, choose the function **Collector and performance DB · Statistics records & file · Online parameters · Dialog step statistics** from the menu bar on the left in administrator mode (see Figure 11.4). Use the instance parameter stat/dbprocrec to define how many of the most resource-intensive COM routines a statistics record of each transaction will be written for. Five is a common setting. Select an instance and adapt the parameter as required. Changes to the parameters will come into effect as soon as you have you have pressed the Save button. You do not need to restart the instance. The change to the parameter will be confirmed by a message in a separate window. Once you have done this, a separate statistics record is created with the precise runtimes for the corresponding number of resource-intensive COM routines in a transaction. You must have Basis Support Package 24 for APO 3.0 or 12 for APO 3.1 to do this.

Given the I/O load caused, writing single statistics records for COM routines is advisable only for specific analysis purposes and only over a short period of time.

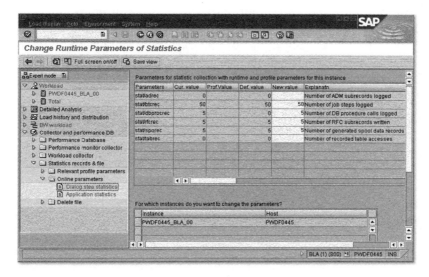

Figure 11.4 Adapting parameter settings for recording statistics

To evaluate these statistics, select transaction **ST03N · Transaction profile**. You will be shown a list of all transactions and report programs that have been run and their response times. Choose the transaction you wish to analyze in greater detail, and select **Single records**. You will be shown the proportional response times for each step in the transaction, including the runtimes of the COM routines. Transaction **STAD** also allows for single record statistics analysis. Single record display is always available only for the current day, however. After a day, the statistics records are consolidated and only total records are kept, because single statistics would occupy too much memory space. This aggregation is carried out by the standard job `COLLECTOR_FOR_PERFORMANCE_MONITOR` on the basis of the report program `RSCOLL00`.

Single record statistics

One advantage of this display is the allocation of COM routine calls to transactions and, thus, applications. Unfortunately there is no where-used list in the APO Data Dictionary for COM routines, as there is for report programs, includes, and tables.

OMS monitor There is an obvious disadvantage to the statistics from transaction **LC10 · liveCache: Monitoring · Problem Analysis · Performance · OMS monitor** (see Figure 11.5). While this transaction does give you an overview of the average response time for each COM routine, including statistics on access, it is not possible to allocate the COM routines to the APO transactions.

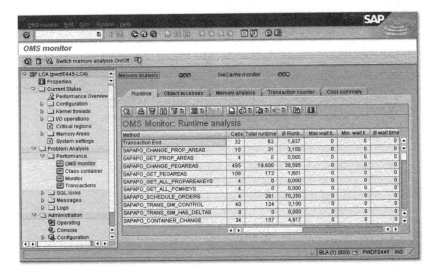

Figure 11.5 Transaction LC10: OMS monitor

11.3 Cache Utilization in the liveCache

The usage of the cache areas is of particular importance for the performance of the liveCache. As with RDBMS, for the liveCache we must assume that there is a starting phase after a restart. In the event of a restart, to speed up the process, at first only part of the data of the active planning version is read in the cache areas. Further data is then read as required. As a result, cache load analysis is meaningful only after around 50,000 COM routine calls. The number of calls executed from the live-Cache is displayed in the statistics in transaction **LC10 · liveCache: Monitoring · Problem Analysis · Performance · Monitor**. The important value here is that given for **External DBPROC calls**. As explained above, COM routines are called with the same syntax as DB procedures, so from a statistics point of view they are counted under **DBPROC calls**. The value for

Internal DBPROC calls refers to the actual calls from DB procedures (stored procedures).

Another important key figure is the number of **Log queue overflows**. This value should be as low as possible. If it is roughly a three-figure sum, this would suggest that there are bottlenecks when writing to the log, and the log queue needs to be extended. The size of the log queue is usually set at 100 pages. You can increase this value using the liveCache parameter LOG_IO_QUEUE (see also Chapter 4).

11.3.1 Data Cache

You can find statistics on the use of the data cache using transaction **LC10 • liveCache: Monitoring • Current status • Memory Areas**. The following rules should be followed:

1. The fill level of the data cache should be well under 100%.
2. The data cache hit rate should be 100%.
3. The ratio of OMS data to OMS history should be around 4:1.

If the data cache is almost 100% full, the hit ratio is less than 100%, and the share of history data in relation to the overall size of the data cache is not 4:1, you should enlarge the data cache. If the share of history data is greater, on the other hand, before enlarging the data cache you should check to see if there are transactional simulations that have been held for too long, and may thus be responsible for the data cache's being so full. Figure 11.6 shows the I/O buffer cache use for a liveCache. In this case, the data cache is only 0.07% full. The ratio between OMS data and OMS history is therefore not very significant. You can check the currently held transactional simulations using transaction **LC10 • liveCache: Monitoring • Problem Analysis • Performance • Monitor • OMS Versions**. There should not be any transactional simulations that are more than 24 hours old. If this is not the case, this means that the maintenance programs /SAPAPO/OM_REORG_DAILY or /SAPAPO/OM_DELETE_OLD_SIMSESS are not executed regularly.

You can determine how much of the memory area is occupied by each individual planning version with transaction **/SAPAPO/OM16**. In the initial screen select **Display planning versions** (see Figure 11.7).

The size of the planning versions

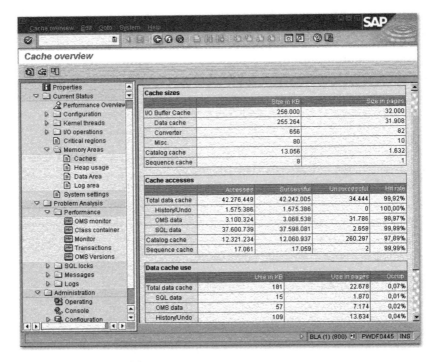

Figure 11.6 Overview of the main memory areas

APO 3.0

For APO release 3.0, this transaction is available from Support Package 16.

Client	Plng versn	Größe (kBy	Client	PlangVersn	Logging	ATP Update	Method	Plng vers.	Model name	Text
		576	001							
001	000	887000	001	000				000	000	ACTIVE YE...
001	MRP	0	001	E1jeVwL1Y.				MRP	MRP	version m...

Figure 11.7 Overview of the planning versions

The actual size of the planning version is calculated by double-clicking on **Calculate** in the **Size** column of the planning version in question. We can differentiate between active and inactive planning versions. Each planning version is administered under a three-digit number. Planning version 000 is always an active planning version. Other planning versions can be generated by copying the data from planning version 000. Depending on whether the planning version created in this way will be used further, or whether it is only for reference purposes, it is either active or inactive. Inactive planning versions are not used in actual planning. (Therefore, it is not very relevant to performance if inactive planning versions are stored on data devspaces.) Which planning versions are active is determined by the relevant departments. The active planning versions as a whole must leave enough memory space available in the data cache; otherwise, there will be read accesses to the hard disk and performance will suffer as a result. This will be reflected in a drop in the data cache hit rate. In this case, the data cache should also be enlarged.

11.3.2 OMS Heap

The OMS heap is used in addition to the data cache in the execution of COM routines. As described in Chapter 6, this memory area is private to each user and is allocated as required. You can use transaction **LC10 • live-Cache: Monitoring • Current status • Memory areas • Heap usage** to get an overview of the maximum OMS heap allocated by COM routines. A more detailed overview of each individual COM routine's heap requirements can be obtained with report program /SAPAPO/OM_LC_MEM_ MONITOR (see Figure 11.8).

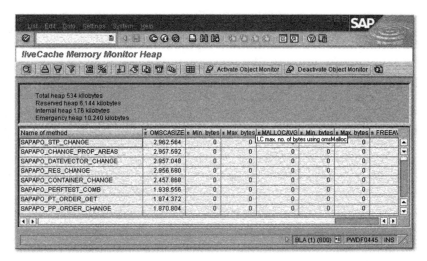

Figure 11.8 List from report program /SAPAPO/OM_LC_MEM_MONITOR

If the COM routines have all claimed the listed memory requirements at the same time, the sum of all the memory requirements will be needed. This event, however, is highly unlikely. The maximum size of the entire

OMS heap reached since the liveCache was restarted is shown by the value **Reserved heap** in the list overview. The sum of all currently used OMS heap is shown by the value for **Total heap**. The maximum OMS heap size available on a server is limited by:

▶ Physically available main memory, which can be reduced by programs running in parallel

▶ Operating system limitations, such as with Windows 32-bit operating systems

▶ The liveCache parameter OMS_HEAP_LIMIT

If the parameter OMS_HEAP_LIMIT is not set explicitly, it is assigned the value 0. In this case, the growth of the OMS heap is not limited by the parameter, and can therefore grow to any size within the physical limits of the server. If the main memory available on the server is insufficient, then the value **R** gets closer to one of the three limits and errors occur in the execution of the COM routines. These errors can have various repercussions. In any case, you will find corresponding entries in the COM trace (transaction **/SAPAPO/OM01**). If the application cannot reduce the data volume to be processed, the only other option is to extend the memory available and, at the same time, raise the parameter OMS_ HEAP_LIMIT.

11.4 Process Overview

Although the statistics discussed thus far always present average values for previous periods, it may also be necessary to analyze the currently active processes. In APO systems as well, the starting point for this is the Process Overview (transactions **SM50** and **SM66**) and the Instance Overview (transaction **SM51**). In the APO system the action *DB Procedure* is also included, which means that a COM routine is executed (see Figure 11.9).

The counterpart of the work process overview is the liveCache task overview, which you can call using transaction **LC10 · liveCache: Console · Active tasks**. If you see a work process with the status *DB Procedure* in the process overview, in the task overview you will find the corresponding task in the status *DcomObjCalled* or *Running* (see Figure 11.10).

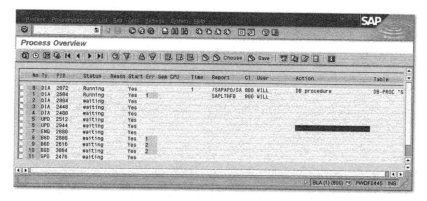

Figure 11.9 Process overview of the APO system

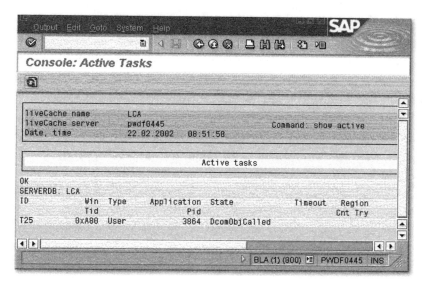

Figure 11.10 Active tasks in the liveCache

The UKTs can have the following status:

▶ *Command Wait*
Task is waiting for requests.

▶ *Running*
Task is processing and needs CPU.

▶ *Runnable*
Task is waiting for a free slot in the thread to continue processing.

▶ *DcomObjCalled*
Task is processing in the coding of a COM routine and needs CPU.

- *IOWait(R)* or *(W)*
  Task is waiting for I/O (Read, Write).

- *Vbegexcl* or *Vsuspend*
  Task is waiting for a lock to be granted.

- *Vwait*
  Task is waiting for an SQL lock that is held by another task—that is to say, ultimately, by an APO user.

Usually the processes should be in the status *Command Wait*, *Running*, *Runnable*, or *DcomObjCalled*. The status *IOWait(R)* or *(W)* in particular, as well as *Vbegexcl* and *Vsuspend*, should last only a very short time. Otherwise, you should assume that there are technical problems.

11.5 Optimizer Statistics for Demand Planning Data

As we have already discussed in Chapter 1, InfoCubes—which you know from BW systems—are used for the management of DP data. The special nature of these data structures must be taken into account when using certain RDBMS with the APO system.

For the database systems IBM DB2/UDB, Oracle and SAP DB, around once a week you should update the optimizer statistics especially for use with BW. To do so, you should schedule the report program SAP_ANALYZE_ALL_INFOCUBES to run once a week. You can find a more detailed explanation in SAPNet Note 421795.

A   liveCache System Tables

Important statistics on the use of the liveCache are managed in system tables. In this way, not only can the statistics be evaluated when using the APO system, but analogue information can also be ascertained with the appropriate SQL queries.

Table	Columns	Command	Output
show_table_def	owner tablename columnname mode datatype len dec columnprivileges ...	`select * from show_tabledef where tablename = '<TABLENAME>'`	Display of the table definition for the table `<TABLENAME>`
db_state		`select * from db_state`	List of all important states in the liveCache
monitor_oms	"Methodname" "SumRuntime" "AvgRuntime" OutOfMemoryExceptions	`select sum ("OutOfMemory-Exceptions") from monitor_oms`	The number of exceptions that have occurred in the allocation of OMS heap due to memory problems
		`select "Method-name" "SumRuntime" "AvgRuntime" from monitor_oms order by "SumRun-time"`	List of COM routine runtimes
monitor		`select * from monitor`	Access statistics
dbparameters		`select * from dbparameters`	liveCache parameters and their settings
versions		`select * from versions`	liveCache release

Table A.1 Important system tables and SELECT commands

Table	Columns	Command	Output
oms_versions	oms_version heap_usage unloaded ...	select oms_ver- sion, heap_usage, unloaded from oms_versions	List of transactional sim-ulations (oms_ver-sion) and their OMS heap requirement (heap_ usage) plus information on whether swap was needed in the cache (unloaded)
sysmon_task_detail	dbid taskname statedesc appl_nodeid appl_process ...	select * from sysmon_task_ detail	Overview of the activities of the liveCache tasks
transactions	transcount write_transaction username connectdate connecttime termed lockmode	select * from transactions	List of all open transac-tions
		select appl_pro- cess, appl_ nodeid, lock- mode, process from sysmon_task_ detail s, trans- actions t where s.dbid = t.pro- cess and lower(t.lock- mode) = 'exclu- sive'	List of all open write transactions and the tasks associated with them
classcontain-ers	pagecount "OCCUPANCY "(%)"	select sum(page- count) from classcontainers	Total number of 8Kb pages (devspaces and cache) occupied by OMS data
		select 100* (1- sum (pagecount* "OCCUPANCY "(%)"/ 100 / sum(page- count))) from classcontainers	Net requirement of OMS data (number of pages occupied that are cleaned up for fragmen-tation)

Table A.1 Important system tables and SELECT commands (continued)

Table	Columns	Command	Output
oms_heap_statistics		`select * from oms_heap_statistics`	Statistics on the usage of OMS heap
serverdbstatistics	**Serverdbsize** **Usedperm** **Unused** **Serverdbfull** **Logsize** **Lognotsaved** **Logsegmentsize** **savepoints** **checkpoints** **maxusedperm** **(from 7.4.3)** ...	`select * from serverdbstatistics`	The size of the liveCache, number of pages occupied, size of the log, size of the log segment, number of savepoints, number of checkpoints, maximum number of pages ever occupied (since release 7.4.3)

Table A.1 Important system tables and SELECT commands (continued)

B Important liveCache Parameters

Table B.1 below presents the most important parameters for the configuration of the liveCache, plus a range of other parameters. Any necessary changes to these parameters are documented in the corresponding SAP-Net Notes.

Meaning	Parameter 7.2 SAPNet Notes 424886 and 433115	Parameter 7.4 SAPNet Notes 496318 and 490958
Size of the data cache in 8Kb pages	DATA_CACHE	CACHE_SIZE
Log mode set	LOG_MODE always DEMO	LOG_MODE currently only SINGLE available
Size of the log queue in pages (default is 100)		LOG_IO_QUEUE
Size of log segment in pages		LOG_SEGMENT_SIZE
Maximum number of log devspaces	MAXARCHIVELOGS irrelevant	MAXARCHIVELOGS
Maximum number of data devspaces	MAXDATADEVSPACES	MAXDATADEVSPACES
Maximum number of 8Kb data pages	MAXDATAPAGES	
Maximum number of backup media to which you can save in parallel	MAXBACKUPDEVS	MAXBACKUPDEVS
Maximum number of SQL locks available in parallel	MAXLOCKS	MAXLOCKS
Maximum wait time allowed for a lock request, in s	REQUEST_TIMEOUT	REQUEST_TIMEOUT
Maximum number of users working simultaneously with the liveCache	MAXUSERTASKS	MAXUSERTASKS
Rundirectory of the live-Cache	RUNDIRECTORY	RUNDIRECTORY
Number of CPUs used	MAXCPU SAPNet Note 410002	MAXCPU SAPNet Note 410002

Table B.1 Important liveCache parameters

Meaning	Parameter 7.2 SAPNet Notes 424886 and 433115	Parameter 7.4 SAPNet Notes 496318 and 490958
Limit on memory requirement, in Kb, for transactional simulations in heap. If a transactional simulation exceeds this limit, at the end of the transaction unchanged data will be deleted from the heap Recommended initial value 2097152	OMS_VERS_THRESHOLD SAPNet Note 419634	OMS_VERS_THRESHOLD SAPNet Note 419634
Percentage of total heap for which excesses are processed as with parameter OMS_VERS_THRESHOLD Recommended initial value 100	OMS_HEAP_THRESHOLD SAPNet Note 419634	OMS_HEAP_THRESHOLD SAPNet Note 419634
Limit for maximum OMS heap that can be claimed (sum of all OMS heaps for each user)	OMS_HEAP_LIMIT SAPNet Note 337445	OMS_HEAP_LIMIT SAPNet Note 337445
Segmenting the OMS heap for the purpose of parallelization in multi-processor environments Recommended initial value 1	OMS_HEAP_COUNT SAPNet Note 457373	OMS_HEAP_COUNT SAPNet Notes 457373 and 516661
Size of related memory blocks in the liveCache heap, in Kb Recommended initial value 10,000	OMS_HEAP_BLOCKCOUNT SAPNet Note 457373	OMS_HEAP_BLOCKCOUNT SAPNet Note 457373

Table B.1 Important liveCache parameters (continued)

The parameters described can be changed either in dialog mode using transaction **LC10** or with the DBMGUI tool. The parameters can also be set on operating system level and remotely. You can find the value of a parameter using the command

```
dbmcli -d <liveCache ID> -n <liveCache Server>
- control,control param_directget <Parametername>
```

To set a parameter, call

```
dbmcli -d <liveCache ID> -n <liveCache Server>
- control,control param_directput <Parametername> <Value>
```

and then directly after it

```
dbmcli -d <liveCache ID> -n <liveCache Server>
- control,control pram_checkall
```

The effect of the last command is that all parameters that depend on a parameter you have set, such as internal parameters, will be re-calculated and adjusted. Changed parameters come into effect after the liveCache has been completely stopped (*offline*) and restarted.

C Important Transactions for the APO System Administrator

The tables below give you an overview of the most important tasks—and the corresponding transaction codes or menu paths—for APO system administration in the dedicated R/3 systems and for the administration of the APO system and its components.

This table offers an outline of useful transactions and reports available in the R/3 system and the APO system for managing the qRFC interface.

Action	Transaction/menu path	Report	Frequency
Customizing inbound scheduler	Transaction **SMQR**		As required
Customizing outbound scheduler	Transaction **SMQRS**		As required
qRFC: Stopping a selected outbound queue	Transaction **SMQ1** or in R/3 systems **Logistics • Central Functions • Supply Chain Planning Interface • Core Interface Advanced Planner and Optimizer • Monitoring • Edit • Execute • Select desired queues • Display selection • Lock or Immediate lock**	RSTRFCQ1	
qRFC: Starting a selected outbound queue	Transaction **SMQ1** or in R/3 systems **Logistics • Central Functions • Supply Chain Planning Interface • Core Interface Advanced Planner and Optimizer • Monitoring • Edit • Execute • Select desired queue • Display selection • Remove lock**	RSTRFCQ3	

Table C.1 Transactions for managing qRFC in R/3 and APO systems

Action	Transaction/menu path	Report	Frequency
qRFC: Monitoring the outbound queue	Transaction **SMQ1** or in R/3 systems **Logistics • Central Functions • Supply Chain Planning Interface • Core Interface Advanced Planner and Optimizer • Monitoring • QRFC Monitor**	RSTRFCQ2	Several times a day
qRFC: Monitoring the inbound queue	Transaction **SMQ2**	RSTRFCI2	Several times a day
qRFC: Stopping a selected inbound queue	Transaction **SMQ2**	RSTRFCI1	
qRFC: Starting a selected inbound queue	Transaction **SMQ2**	RSTRFCI3	

Table C.1 Transactions for managing qRFC in R/3 and APO systems (continued)

Action	Transaction/menu path	Report	Frequency
Defining the Integration Model Menu of the qRFC monitor and the application log	Transaction **CFM1** or **Logistics • Central Functions • Supply Chain Planning Interface • Core Interface Advanced Planner and Optimizer • Integration model • Generate • Create and activate**	RIMODGEN	Necessary during implementation and in the event of any changes
Generating and activating the integration model (starting the initial data transfer)		Scheduling the background job: RIMODGEN-Generation RIMODAC2-Activation	As the application requires

Table C.2 Transactions in R/3 systems

Action	Transaction/menu path	Report	Frequency
Checking the integration model	Transaction **CFM4** or **Logistics · Central Functions · Supply Chain Planning Interface · Core Interface Advanced Planner and Optimizer · Integration model · Generate · Display**		
Changing the integration model	Transaction **CFM6** or **Logistics · Central Functions · Supply Chain Planning Interface · Core Interface Advanced Planner and Optimizer · Integration model · Generate · Display**		
Deleting obsolete integration models		RIMODDEL	Weekly
Checking the data transfer method	Transaction **CFC5**		
Selecting and adjusting message types for change transfer	Transaction **BD50**		
Activating change pointers	Transaction **BD61**		
Reorganizing change pointers	Transaction **BD22** or **Tools · ALE Administration · Services · Change pointers · Reorganization**		At least once a week
Starting the data transfer for change data using change pointers	Transaction **CFP1**	Scheduling the background job RCPTRAN4	As the application requires

Table C.2 Transactions in R/3 systems (continued)

Action	Transaction/menu path	Report	Frequency
Making settings for application logging	Transaction **CFG1** or **Logistics • Central Functions • Supply Chain Planning Interface • Core Interface Advanced Planner and Optimizer • Monitoring • Application log • Display entries**		If required
Deleting the application log	Transaction **CFGD** or **Logistics • Central Functions • Supply Chain Planning Interface • Core Interface Advanced Planner and Optimizer • Monitoring • Application log • Delete entries**	`sbal_delete`	Daily after checking
Activating debugging	Transaction **CFC2** or **Logistics • Central Functions • Supply Chain Planning Interface • Settings • User parameters**		
Defining and allocating the logical system to the client	Transaction **SALE**		During the implementation phase
Monitoring/starting/stopping data channel for master data	Transaction **CFP2**	Report RCPQUEUE	As required

Table C.2 Transactions in R/3 systems (continued)

Action	Transaction/menu path	Report	Frequency
qRFC: Outbound alert monitor	Transaction **/SAPAPO/CW** or **Tools • APO Administration • Monitor • QRFC Alert**	`/SAPAPO/RCIF-QUEUECHECK`	Schedule every 15 minutes
qRFC: Inbound alert monitor	Transaction **/SAPAPO/CQINW**	`/SAPAPO/RCIFIN-QUEUECHECK`	Schedule every 15 minutes

Table C.3 Transactions in the APO system

Action	Transaction/menu path	Report	Frequency
Activating application logging	Transaction **/SAPAPO/C3** or Transaction **SMQ1** or **Tools • APO Administration • Monitor • Application log • Switch on logging**		As required
Checking the entries in the application log	Transaction **/SAPAPO/C3** or **Tools • APO Administration • Monitor • Application log • Display entries**		Regularly, at least once a day
Deleting the entries in the application log	Transaction **/SAPAPO/C3** or Transaction **SMQ1** or **Tools • APO Administration • Monitor • Application log • Delete entries**	/SAPAPO/RDELLOG	Once a day in the background, after checking
Activating the debug option in APO	Transaction **/SAPAPO/C4**		When analyzing error situations
Defining and allocating the logical system to the client	Transaction **SALE** or **Tools • Business Engineer • Customizing • SAP Reference IMG • APO Implementation Guide • R/3 Basis Customizing • Application Link Enabling (ALE) • Prepare sending and receiving systems • Set up logical systems**		
SCM queue manager	Transaction **/SAPAPO/CQ**		

Table C.3 Transactions in the APO system (continued)

Action	Transaction/menu path	Report	Frequency
Defining the business system group	Transaction /SAPAPO/C1 or Tools • Business Engineer • Customizing • SAP Reference IMG • APO Implementation Guide • R/3 Basis Customizing • Advanced Planner and Optimizer • Basis Settings • Maintain business system group		During the implementation phase
Allocating the logical system to the operating system group	Transaction /SAPAPO/C2		
Checking the external consistency between the APO system and each dedicated R/3 system	Transaction /SAPAPO/CCR	/SAPAPO/CIF_ DELTAREPORT3	
Checking the internal consistency of the APO system (APO DB ↔ live-Cache)	Transaction /SAPAPO/OM17		If errors occur in the application, after non-complete recoveries
Checking the internal consistency of Demand Planning data		/SAPAPO/TS_LCM_ CONS_CHECK_ALL	If errors occur in the application, after non-complete recoveries
Checking the internal consistency and, if required, repairing individual planning areas in DP		/SAPAPO/TS_LCM_ CONS_CHECK	If errors occur, after non-complete recoveries

Table C.3 Transactions in the APO system (continued)

Action	Transaction/menu path	Report	Frequency
Periodically reorganizing COM objects		/SAPAPO/OM_ REORG_ DAILY	Daily in the background
Periodically maintaining transactional simulations		/SAPAPO/OM_SIM-SESS	Every half hour
liveCache administration and monitoring	Transaction **LC10** or **Tools • APO Administration • liveCache/COM routines • Monitor**		
Configuring live-Cache parameters, devspaces, etc.	Transaction **LC10 • liveCache: Console**		As required
liveCache monitoring processes and memory management	Transaction **LC10 • liveCache: Console**		Several times a day
Monitoring COM routines, cache sizes, and SQL statement statistics for the liveCache	Transaction **LC10 • liveCache: Monitoring**		Daily
Monitoring liveCache performance	Transaction **LC10 • liveCache: Monitoring • Problem analysis • Performance**		Daily
Maintaining liveCache connections	Transaction **LC10 • Integration •**		As required
Checking the operativeness of the liveCache	**Tools • APO Administration • liveCache/COM-Routines • Tools • liveCache Test Program • Start liveCache Check**	/SAPAPO/OM_ LCCHECK	After installation, upgrades, or support packages, or for error analysis

Table C.4 Transactions in the APO system for the administration of the liveCache

Action	Transaction/menu path	Report	Frequency
Checking live-Cache connection status and COM routines		/SAPAPO/OM_ LIVE_ CACHE_ STATUS	After installation, upgrades, or support packages, or for error analysis
liveCache 7.2: Switching logging on or off	Transaction **/SAPAPO/OM06** or **Tools • APO Administration • liveCache/COM routines • Recovery • Set logging level**	/SAPAPO/OM_LC_ LOGGING_SET	If required in error analysis
liveCache 7.2: Planning a periodical job to write checkpoints	Transaction **/SAPAPO/OM18** or **Tools • APO Administration • liveCache/COM routines • Tools • Checkpoint**	/SAPAPO/OM_ CHECKPOINT_ WRITE	Background job, recommended frequency: 2–6 hours
liveCache 7.2: Deleting the job to write checkpoints		/SAPAPO/OM_ CHECKPOINT_ UNPLAN	As required
liveCache 7.2: Checking the consistency of log areas		/SAPAPO/OM_LC_ LOGAREA_CHECK	After unscheduled termination
Protocol of logging options and written checkpoints	Transaction **/SAPAPO/OM11**		As required
Deleting the protocol of logging options and written checkpoints	Transaction **/SAPAPO/OM12**		As required, about once a week, after checking
liveCache 7.2: Recovery	**Tools • APO Administration • liveCache/COM routines • Recovery**	/SAPAPO/OM_LC_ RECOVERY	If required
liveCache 7.2: Displaying the recovery log		/SAPAPO/OM09	After a recovery

Table C.4 Transactions in the APO system for the administration of the liveCache (continued)

Action	Transaction/menu path	Report	Frequency
Deleting the anchor tables		/SAPAPO/DELETE_ LC_ANCHORS	Should be done during the live-Cache initialization process, transaction LC10
Activating trace for COM routines	Transaction **/SAPAPO/OM02**		To analyze error situations
Displaying the trace for COM routines	Transaction **/SAPAPO/OM01**		To analyze error situations
Displaying the COM routine version	Transaction **/SAPAPO/OM04**		As required
liveCache data browser Size of planning versions	Transaction **/SAPAPO/OM16**		For analyzing error situations and for estimating space requirements

Table C.4 Transactions in the APO system for the administration of the liveCache (continued)

Action	Transaction/menu path	Report	Frequency
Optimizer log	Transaction **/SAPAPO/OPT11**		Regularly, after optimization runs
Displaying the optimizer user list	Transaction **/SAPAPO/OPT03**		As required
Displaying the version	Transaction **/SAPAPO/OPT09**		As required
Displaying the processes	Transaction **/SAPAPO/OPT12**		As required

Table C.5 Transactions in the APO system for the administration of APO optimizers

Action	Transaction/menu path	Report	Frequency
Maintaining the master data for the optimization server	**Tools • Business Engineer • Customizing • SAP Reference IMG • APO Implementation Guide • R/3 Basis Customizing • Advanced Planner and Optimizer • Basis Settings • Optimization • Basic functions • Maintain master data for the optimization server**		During implementation
Deleting the application data after a set number of days	Transaction **/SAPAPO/COPT00** or **Tools • Business Engineer • Customizing • SAP Reference IMG • APO Implementation Guide • R/3 Basis Customizing • Advanced Planner and Optimizer • Basis Settings • Optimization • Basic functions • Maintaining master data for the optimization server**		During implementation
Checking the availability of the optimization server	Transaction **/SAPAPO/COPT00**		During implementation
Customizing the optimizers	Transaction **/SAPAPO/COPT01**		During implementation
Customizing the PP/DS optimizer	Transaction **/SAPAPO/COPT02**		During implementation
Defining and checking the RFC connections to optimizers	Transaction **SM59**		During implementation

Table C.5 Transactions in the APO system for the administration of APO optimizers (continued)

D   Frequent Periodic Background Jobs

To guarantee the operation of APO and R/3 systems, a number of periodic background jobs should be scheduled. The following table gives an overview of important background jobs that should be run regularly in R/3 systems to transfer data to an allocated APO system.

Role	Report	Period
Generating integration models	RIMODGEN	Defined by the application team
Activating integration models	RIMODAC4	Defined by the application team
Initialization of the transfer of plannable products, work centers, classes, and characteristics.	RIMODINI	Defined by the application team
Initialization of the transfer of production process models (PPM)	RSPPMCHG	Defined by the application team
Deleting obsolete integration models	RIMODDEL	There should be no more than 2–3 old integration models
Incremental data transfer of master data	RCPTRAN4	Defined by the application team, if BTEs are used
Deleting obsolete change pointers	RBDCPCLR	Run weekly to delete those more than 14 days old, if BTEs are used
Deleting application log	SBAL_DELETE	Weekly, after discussing with the application team

Table D.1 Background jobs in R/3 systems for data transfer

Special background jobs are scheduled in APO systems for maintaining the system. The following table gives an overview of these jobs.

Role	Report	Period
QRFC outbound alert monitor	/SAPAPO/RCIFQUEUECHECK	Every 15 minutes
QRFC inbound alert monitor	/SAPAPO/RCIFINQUEUECHECK	Every 15 minutes

Table D.2 Background jobs for maintaining the APO system

Role	Report	Period
Deleting application log	`SBAL_DELETE`	Weekly, after discussing with the application team
liveCache 7.2: Writing a checkpoint	`/SAPAPO/OM_CHECKPOINT_WRITE`	As required, every 2–6 hours
Deleting obsolete transactional simulations, and the like	`/SAPAPO/OM_REORG_DAILY`	Daily
Deleting transactional simulations that have not been allocated	`/SAPAPO/OM_DELETE_OLD_SIM-SESS`	Every 30 minutes
Deleting logs from Demand Planning, if logging is used (SAPNet Note 512184)	`/SAPAPO/TS_BATCH_LOGFILE`	Daily, with the option of deleting all logs that are more than one week old
Loading data from an InfoCube to a planning area	`/SAPAPO/RTSINPUT_CUBE`	As required

Table D.2 Background jobs for maintaining the APO system (continued)

E   Menu Tree of Transaction LC10

The following diagrams should give you an idea of the structure and functions of transaction **LC10** for liveCache administration. The menu trees show the structure of the transaction in APO 3.1 and APO 3.0 from Basis Support Package 30. Transaction **LC10** forms part of the SAP software Basis. The transaction is therefore also available in R/3 systems 4.6D and 4.6C from Basis Support Package 30.

liveCache: Integration

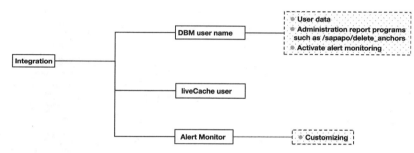

Figure E.1 liveCache: Integration

liveCache: Console and Alert Monitor

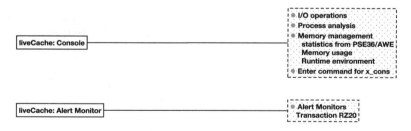

Figure E.2 liveCache: Console and alert monitor

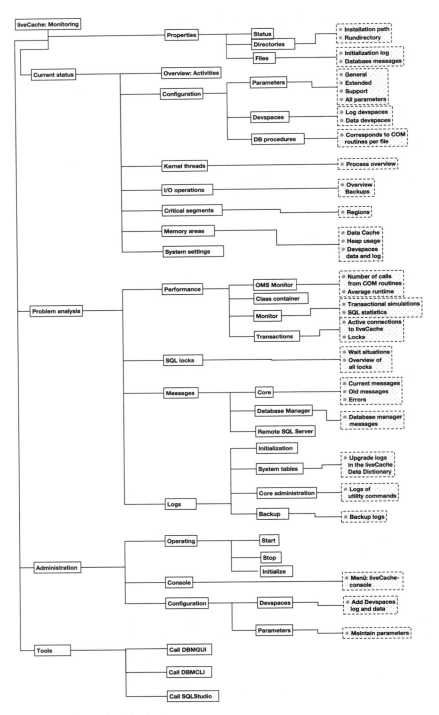

Figure E.3 liveCache: Monitoring

F Contents and Implementation of the CD

The accompanying CD is divided into the following directories:

▶ *SoluManRoadmap*
Solution Management Roadmap

▶ *BestPractice*
Best Practice documents

▶ *SMAP*
System Maintenance Action Plan

F.1 Solution Management Roadmap

When you implement a software solution, a well-structured, coordinated procedure is always required. SAP's Standard Implementation method is available in *AcceleratedSAP*. This solution includes roadmaps which assign the different project phases based on different aspects, project tasks, services, Best Practice documents, and so on. The target groups for the roadmaps are project managers, employees, and consultants. The technical Solution Management Roadmap available on this CD deals with the procedure for implementing the technical infrastructure and operating the SAP software.

Installation and Start

The Solution Management Roadmap can be installed on Windows systems. The following files are included on the CD:

▶ *roadmap_description.pdf*
Documentation on using the Roadmap, which can be read with *Acrobat Reader*

▶ *roadmap.zip*
A compressed file of the roadmap components

You will need *WinZip* and a Web browser to install the roadmap. Open the archive by double-clicking on the file *roadmap.zip*. Extract all the components to a directory created especially for this purpose on your PC, such as *roadmap*. In this directory, a new directory called *SAP_RM_HTM* will be created and filled with files and two further directories. After unzipping, you can open the roadmap by double-clicking on the file *Index.htm* in the sub-directory *SAP_RM_ HTM*.

Operation

After starting the roadmap, a window opens, in which the individual implementation steps are presented in a navigation tree in the area to the left. If you click on selected themes, the corresponding information, documents, links to SAP Web pages, and so on are displayed on the right.

F.2　Best Practice Documents

The *Best Practice documents* deal with key aspects of the operation of mySAP Business Suite. For each theme, the basic principles and know-how for optimum operation are presented. The documents are available in PDF format. They can be opened using *Acrobat Reader*.

F.3　System Maintenance Action Plan (SMAP)

SMAP is a document in PDF format that contains a collection of all the necessary work and tasks involved in the administration of an APO system. It has to be specially adapted depending on the business process and customer situation. SMAP can serve as a basis for a management instruction manual. The document also provides a summary of the APO-specific tasks described in this book.

There are two versions of SMAP available on CD: SMAP_72 is for APO systems with liveCache version 7.2, SMAP_74 for those with liveCache version 7.4.

G   List of Abbreviations

The most important abbreviations used in this book are explained briefly below.

Term	Explanation
ALE	Application Link Enabling
APO	Advanced Planner and Optimizer
APS	Advanced Planning and Scheduling
BAPI	Business Application Programming Interface
BDC	Backup Domain Controller
BW	Business Information Warehouse
BOM	Bill of Material
CDP	Characteristic Dependent Planning
CIF	Core Interface
CPFR	Collaborative Planning, Forecasting, and Replenishment
CRM	Customer Relationship Management
CRP	Continuous Replenishment Programs
CRT	Conflict Resolution Transport
CTM	Capable-to-Match
DHCP	Dynamic Host Configuration Protocol
DP	Demand Planning
DS	Detailed Scheduling
EDI	Electronic Data Interchange
ERP	Enterprise Resource Planning
GATP	Global Available-to-Promise
IPPE	Integrated Production and Process Engineering
ITS	Internet Transaction Server
IDES	Internet Demonstration and Education System
LCMS	liveCache Management System
MRP	Material Resource Planning

Table G.1 Important abbreviations

Term	Explanation
OMS	Object Management System
OCX	Object Component Extension
PDC	Primary Domain Controller
PLM	Product Lifecycle Management
POS	Planning Object Structure or, in SD, also Point of Sale
PP	Production Planning
PPM	Production Process Model
SCC	Supply Chain Cockpit
SCM	Supply Chain Management
SCOPE	Supply Chain Optimization, Planning, and Execution
SFA	Sales Force Automation
SNP	Supply Network Planning
VICS	Voluntary Inter-Industry Commerce Standards
VMI	Vendor Managed Inventory
VS	Vehicle Scheduling

Table G.1 Important abbreviations (continued)

H   Bibliography

[Bartsch 2002]: Bartsch, Helmut; Bickenbach, Peter. *Supply Chain Management mit SAP APO*. SAP PRESS, Bonn 2002.

[Brand 1999]: Brand, Hartwig. *SAP R/3-Einführung mit ASAP*. SAP PRESS, Bonn 1999.

[Hagemann/Will 2003]: Hagemann, Sigrid; Will, Liane. *SAP R/3 System Administration, 3rd Ed*. SAP PRESS, New York 2003.

[McFarland Metzger 2000]: McFarland Metzger, Sue; Röhrs, Susanne. *SAP R/3 Change and Transport Management. The official SAP Guide*. Sybex, 2000.

[Read 2002]: Read, Paul. *SAP Database Administration with Microsoft SQL Server 2000*. SAP PRESS, Bonn 2002.

[SAP DB Docu Messages]: SAP. *Messages: SAP DB 7.2 and 7.3*. Walldorf 2002.

[SAP DB Docu SQL Studio 2002]: SAP. *SQL Studio: SAP DB 7.3*. Walldorf 2002.

[SAP DB Docu DBMCLI]: SAP. *Summary of DBMCLI Commands*. Walldorf 2002.

[SAPLabs 2002]: SAP Labs. *SAP Guide System Administration*. SAP Labs, Palo Alto 2000.

[Schneider 2002]: Schneider, Thomas. *SAP Performance Optimization Guide*. SAP PRESS, New York 2002.

Index